Making Him

L.O.R.D.

Living Out Reproducible
Discipleship

Guy Caskey

7710-T Cherry Park Drive, Ste 224
Houston, TX 77095
713-766-4271
www.WorldwidePublishingGroup.com

Paperback: 978-1-68411-276-0
Hardcover: 978-1-365-82578-1

Published in the United States of America

Table of Contents

Acknowledgements

Thank you Jesus for changing my life! You have been so faithful to me.

I want to thank my family for their support. Kelli, words can't express the appreciation, and love I have for you. You have demonstrated incredible strength, sacrifice, and service. I am grateful for you.

I want to give a big shout out to Kristin Funderburg and her tireless work on editing, illustrating and contributing to this work. I am proud to have you as a spiritual daughter, and you amaze me! Thanks so much for your love, and faithfulness all of these years.

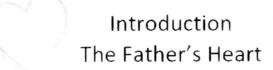

Introduction
The Father's Heart

Making Him LORD is a book about allowing God to control your life in such a way that there are incredible results. "You know, brothers and sisters, that our visit with you was not without results." 1 Thessalonians 2:1

The Bible refers to results as Christ expressing His life in and through you. Some may refer to this as fruit, work, multiplication or movement. All of those are appropriate ways to describe how God wants to cover the earth with His Glory.[1]

From the very beginning, we want to be honest with the admission that this cannot be done on our own, but can only be done by Christ's power! A life surrendered to God is a vessel used by God to accomplish His vision.

L.O.R.D. is an acrostic that stands for Living Out Reproducible Discipleship. If you want your life to echo throughout the halls of eternity, this is a book for you. Our Master and King has set forth the plan, and people of purpose are His chosen instruments.

---

[1] Habbakuk 2:14

This book is about a captivating vision held by many Kingdom-minded citizens who desire that none shall perish. This is the Father's heart!

From Genesis to Revelation we see that the Father's heart is for all nations. The Father has been about the transformation of hearts from generation to generation. When He touches hearts, the fruit of His transformation (life change) is multiplication from one generation to the next. This is the stuff His Kingdom is made of!

I hope you will press in and obey Christ our King, who will take us by the hand and lead us to a God we can call Father. May His vision and love compel you until there is no place left where the Gospel has not been proclaimed by reproducing churches, so that His glory fills the earth!

Chapter 1

Why Has God Placed Us Here?

(Big Enough Vision to Think Small)

What if it is true that there is a kingdom of darkness and a kingdom of light? What if the kingdom of light can only be seen when you Pledge Allegiance to its King? What if we really are living in a matrix or there really is a wardrobe that we must walk through to enter Aslan's world?[i]

If it is true, then there is significance in every breath we take and every choice we make.

I believe that it is true from my own personal experience, and from the witness of millions of others. When I made Jesus Lord of my life, it changed me and I discovered a deeper reality. Just like the story of the man in John 9, I too can say, "I was blind but now I see."

There was a time when I blindly served the kingdom of darkness; but now, with vision, I serve the kingdom of light. Making Him Lord has brought a deep change in me. I have a deep sense of mission. Suffering here brings a sense of joy that can only be described as being from another place – it's eternal.

I have discovered that there are many others who are also passionately pursuing the King! They are my family; and we serve our King, His mission, and one another. We ask you to join us on the journey of making Him LORD!

"This is your last chance. After this, there is no turning back. You take the blue pill -- the story ends, you wake up in your bed and believe whatever

1

you want to believe. You take the red pill -- you stay in Wonderland and I show you how deep the rabbit hole goes."

~ Morpheus in the Matrix[ii]

In this first chapter, we're going to talk about how we can make Him LORD by living out the Great Commission. My hope is to encourage you and me to have a vision for seeing Christ's life multiplied. When we talk about making Him L.O.R.D. we are referring to Living Out Reproducible Discipleship. We will discuss the meaning of multiplication, how it relates to the Great Commission, and ultimately how it relates to our eternal purpose. We want to look at the question, "Why has God placed us here?"

God has a plan for every one of us, and His plan is for us to join Him. Often, we act as though that plan is us getting to do what we want, and asking God to put his stamp of approval on it; but God has said clearly through His Word that He already has a plan, and He wants us to join Him. I believe we need to be doing those things that Jesus said we need to do, rather than pursuing our own agendas. We need to make Him LORD!

What we want to do is encourage one another to obey Christ. We need to stop simply talking about it; but do it in our words, our deeds, our actions, and the attitudes of our hearts. One of the things I am confident of is that you and I can do these things because Christ empowers us to do them. This confidence comes from 2 Peter 1:3 which says, "His divine power has given us everything we need for a godly life, through our knowledge of Him who called us by His own glory and goodness." This verse assures us that God will not ask or call us into anything that he hasn't promised to do in and through us.

We've got the power because the power is in Him. Following Jesus and making disciples must come from a surrendered heart. We simply need to say, "God, here I am. Use me. I'm trusting

2

You and want to be used. Teach me. Thank You for loving me." We are not alone in carrying these things out. It all flows out of Him working through us because we are in Him and He is in us. He wants to use us, so we need to trust the promise He gave us in the Great Commission when He said, "I will be with you always."

Learning how to trust, or abide, in Christ is essential if we are going to produce abundant fruit that lasts. Please take some time to look at John 15. Reflect on it and ask yourself, "What's it gonna take?" (Some call this a WIGTake.)

In making disciples, there needs to be one-on-one discipleship, but there are times we need discipleship in a community setting. We need what we call 'missional communities', which are churches that are about trusting (abiding) in Him and helping others learn to trust Him. That is what this book is about.

We have the power, and the power is in Him. When you recognize that you have power, you are like dynamite. His dynamic Spirit is explosive in you as you learn to trust Him and be used by Him. This is a very important thing for us to keep in mind. I don't know about you, but personally, being a hard charger, I had to learn that I can't do this by pulling myself up by my own bootstraps. I've learned that it's about trusting Him. We have the power because the power is in Christ and Christ is in us.

While this book is not intended to be a full-fledged workbook, we know it may be utilized to train groups. There will be times that we provide a practice activity, which can be done as an individual or a group. If you are reading through this book as a group/church of more than five people, we recommend splitting into multiple smaller groups to encourage full participation from everyone. It may be helpful to select one person in each smaller group as a reporter to note the discussion and share with the larger group. Practice activities will be noted to help guide group work.

Practice Activity:

Take five or six minutes to discuss when Jesus told the 12 disciples, in Acts 1, to wait for the promise of the Father; and when the power comes in Acts 2. The disciples had been literally walking with Jesus, but I think there's a clear difference when the power came into their lives after He left.

- Look at Acts 1:8. How did the disciples act before Jesus told them, "I'm going to give you power and you shall be my witnesses when my power comes on you?"

- Look at Acts 2. How did the disciples act differently when they received the power?

Here's a little encouragement if you haven't read completely through the Bible or feel that you don't have much Bible knowledge. There's great benefit to working together as a group. Everybody has a unique perspective. If each person will share whatever they observe, it will provide a fuller picture of the topic of discussion.

Obedient Faith

The disciples had all kinds of convincing proofs, but they didn't have the power until after the Holy Spirit came. The question we should ask ourselves is, "Do we believe we have the same power?" I believe we do. Another question to ask is, "Do we have the courage and the boldness to trust Christ?" We have all His resources available to us, so are we going to live this stuff out?

We will only be able to live it out by His power, and that's the whole point we're trying to get across. The disciples became a new creation, and the change in their heart was so foreign that it blew people away. The change was reflected in their attitudes and actions, as they no longer saw a distinction between Greek and Jew. That's very important.

Now, after the Holy Spirit came, were these guys perfect? Hardly! In fact, we see a lot of mistakes, and we see a lot of learning. That's the other cool side about it to me, that we can see these guys learning. One of the things I like to talk about is how, throughout Paul's missionary journeys, you can see him adjusting, learning, and even changing his strategy along the way as he matured.

I love that!

I love that in the first journey to the Galatian region, it was almost like he had this sense of urgency to get to as many places as he could, as quickly as possible. They ran from one place to the next planting churches; but they didn't establish leaders, which meant they were constantly going back to that region to try to re-affirm and re-strengthen.

When he went on the second journey, he made some changes by taking a bunch of guys with him and dropping them off. However, from my observation, it appears that the Galatian region needed more follow up and strengthening in comparison to Macedonia and Asia. I think Paul is learning how to develop an apostolic band or a team that can successfully catalyze a church planting movement throughout a region. We would call this a "No Place Left" vision.

Next, we read, in Acts 19, about a school in Tyrannus where Paul finds the indigenous people of Ephesus. He asks them if they know the power of the Holy Spirit, because he noticed there was something not right about the way they were functioning together. When they respond that they do not know, he tells them about the power available through the Holy Spirit. They believe and receive the Holy Spirit, and he then begins training them.

As a result, all of Asia hears the good news! This is truly significant when we consider that the book of Revelation is addressed to the seven churches in Asia. Out of Paul's adjustment, training, learning, and maturing as a spiritual father and leader in his apostolic role, we can see the extent of the impact.

So, these guys weren't perfect. They were learning just like we need to be learning. They had to deal with working through conflict with one another just as we do. Consider the conflicts between Paul and Barnabas or Paul and Peter. Just like us, these men are in process, and friction is essential for them to become the precious stones that lay the foundation for the living temple that God is building together. We are under construction and the Father has promised to build us into something beautiful if we will trust His design.[2]

The whole premise of the idea we want to present with discipleship is simply that we need to be growing to be more and more like Christ. The more we obediently walk in what we know, the more we grow and learn; and the more we grow and learn, the more effective we will be at helping others grow and accomplish this great mission.

It is worth noting that multiplication does indeed happen in all three regions (Galatia, Macedonia and Asia) of Paul's Journeys. I personally believe that the Asian movement was more effective due to Paul's maturity and him learning about the power of the Spirit working through effective tools. One of the tools we need to sharpen is vision casting.

---

[2] 1 Peter 2:4-10; Ephesians 2:10

Having A Big Enough Vision to Think Small

What exactly does it mean to have a big enough vision to think small? Think about this. Jesus is the son of God - perfect, holy, filled with the Holy Spirit, has all the gifts, has everything. He did minister to many, but He invested and poured His life into just 12. Even within those 12, He seemed to have three or four that He spent more time with as well. You and I are here today because the Author, the Perfecter of our faith, the Chief Apostle, the first Sent One by God came and had a big enough vision to think small.

His vision is seen in Acts 1:8 which says, "But you will receive power when the Holy Spirit comes on you; and you will be my witnesses in Jerusalem, and in all Judea and Samaria, and to the ends of the earth." In this, we see that He starts out in one location, then moves to a bigger one and a bigger one, until the vision is that the whole earth would hear the good news about Jesus Christ. But He started in one location with a few.

Now, there's an interesting verse about God's eternal purpose that I don't hear taught very much in our culture. Ephesians 3:10 tells us that God has had an eternal purpose, which means forever, long before this earth was created, before time was created. I believe that purpose is to see a body of Christ gathering reveal who He is in every city on the face of the planet. God wants to see the body of Christ growing and expressing His life.

Jesus even expressed to His disciples that it was important for Him to leave so that they would be doing greater things than Him through the power of the Holy Spirit. He is going to invade Body of Christ Gatherings. God is going to give them gifts; and use them to multiply disciples, and transform entire communities.

He wants to see the whole world reached. It may feel a little overwhelming, and we might wonder if we should consider it our job to reach the whole world. The answer is both yes and no. Our job is to reach the areas where God has placed us as we're going day to day; and He will use the reproduction of our obedience to reach the whole world.

In John 15, Jesus said He is the vine and we are the branches. He is the tree of life! He wants to see a tree of Life, a local church, planted in every tribe, tongue, and peoples on the face of the planet.

So far in this chapter, we've discussed the big picture, the vision; and the fact that you and I, by the power of God, can accomplish what He's asked us to do. Remember, there is nothing He has called us to do that He hasn't promised to do in and through us, and He's asked us to go and make disciples.

He has asked us like Habakkuk to take the vision, write it down, and run with it until the Glory of the Lord covers the entire earth. Go therefore and make disciples of all nations.[3]

We have to start with the end in mind. The end in mind is God's big vision to reach the whole world; and that will happen as we think small, and begin being obedient right where we are. In 2 Timothy 2:2, this same idea of having a big enough vision to think small is modeled by Paul.

Paul said, "Follow me as I follow Christ."[4] He was emphasizing the importance of modeling a life that follows Christ, rather than just teaching to gather listeners. Looking back at 2 Timothy 2:2, Paul addresses Timothy as his son in the faith. He instructs Timothy to pour his life into faithful ones, just as Paul had poured into him, who will obediently pour their lives

---

[3] Matthew 28:19
[4] 1 Corinthians 11:1

into others. For God's big vision in Acts 1:8, for His children to extend to the ends of the earth, we have to take the necessary small steps that Paul is teaching Timothy here.

Elephants and Rabbits

Culturally, I think we tend to embrace addition and subtraction rather than multiplication. One example I use to cast the vision about multiplication is the comparison between an elephant and a rabbit.

Let's just say the elephants start out with a vision, and their vision is to reach the world by multiplying elephants. So, we put two elephants in the perfect environment to raise a family of elephants. It is important to note that an elephant must wait 10 – 20 years to be sexually mature. Now, once we wait 10 – 20 years, and we place a beautiful lady elephant and a good looking male elephant in the perfect environment, how long do you think it would take those two elephants to begin a family?

It would take longer than two years before they could become a family of three elephants. The gestation period of an elephant is two years, and then it takes four or five more years for them to have another baby. Let's say the best case scenario is that a family can be started by elephants in three years. Now elephants are big, and they are beautiful; but are we going to be able to take over the world with elephants very fast? I'd say not.

Okay, let's take a look at rabbits. There are even things that multiply more rapid than a rabbit, such as seeds or mice; but let's stick with our little, furry friends, the rabbits. Using the same scenario, we put them in the best environment possible for them to start their rabbit family.

Rabbits become sexually mature within six to eight weeks, which is much faster than an elephant, and they have multiple babies. In the three years, it took to get the elephant family to reach three elephants, how many rabbits do you think there would be? Typically, when this question is asked in trainings, nobody ever comes close to guessing the correct number.

I'm no computation expert or mathematician; but many people have tried to work the math, and the number comes out to be something around 476 million. That is with no deaths, no predators, etc.; but 476 million rabbits in just three years is a lot!

Now, let's put this in our context. If we view the church as a very large building where we are providing religious goods for Christian consumers, and our mentality is 'come grow with us'; how easily or quickly would we be able to reproduce something like that in other cultures, such as the sands of Somalia?

There are not many people who could actually lead and multiply something like that. I'm not doggin' elephants or churches with large buildings. They are beautiful creations, but I'm just telling you that they do not multiply very quickly or easily.

The most common mindset we have in America is that the church is a building with all kinds of programs, rather than people living out a mission.

I can confidently say that there are 'rabbit' groups, or disciple-making groups, that exist and can be reproduced and multiplied from here all the way to the sands of Somalia. I know this because I'm part of it, and we are seeing churches multiplied in the sands of Somalia. Personally, I'm convinced this is the only way we're going to be able to reach the bigger vision. We must have a big enough vision to think small. We are sent ones!

From the Fold to the Field

As I mentioned earlier, we are not against buildings. We need existing facilities and church buildings to be sending bases, equipping centers, and gathering points. The point we want to make is just that there should be an element of going, just like when Jesus talks about getting out of the fold and into the fields in John 10 and Luke 10.

We can't have a "four walls" mentality. We've got to get out there. The following chapters are going to further discuss those small steps we must take in order to partner with God in His vision for the whole world to know Him.

We're going to provide you with specific tools that will help you effectively do all of this. We don't claim that these are the only or best tools; however, we want to give you something that has been working for us in the case that you don't have anything. They have also been proven to be effective even in remote cultures; so, they can be used both here and there in order to multiply disciples.

The Fourth Generation

One of the other cool things I love about 2 Timothy 2:2 is how we see the vision being lived out from Paul to Timothy to faithful ones to others, which is four generations. This is powerful imagery that takes us back to the Old Testament where it talks about the sins of the fathers being handed down to the third generation. I believe once we start seeing multiplication of discipleship to the fourth generation, where these "others" are multiplying disciples, we will see curses broken; and the transformation of communities will organically begin to take shape.

However, if we continue to believe that discipleship is a program, and what we want rather than what He wants; then we will continue to be stuck in the kind of stuff that we're currently stuck in here in our nation and culture.

Let's revisit our comparison between addition and multiplication. One of the potentially misleading things about addition is that in the early stages, it does increase faster than multiplication. Look at the chart below that reveals the clear difference between addition and multiplication.

+		X
1 + 1 = 2	>	1 × 1 = 1
2 + 2 = 4	=	2 × 2 = 4
3 + 3 = 6	<	3 × 3 = 9
4 + 4 = 8	2x	4 × 4 = 16

You can see how, in the early stages, addition is faster; but over time, multiplication takes off. If you and I were to invest in one, two, or three people, and they began to invest in one or two others; imagine the difference there will be as we release them and bless them to go and do likewise - to multiply and reproduce.

Imagine the transformation that would result in our world if we obediently followed this principle of multiplication! The role of an apostle is to be a culture changer, but we have forgotten some of the apostolic patterns, such as multiplication. We have forgotten the ways of Jesus, who is our chief apostle.

The Four Soils

It should be clear to see by now that there is a significant need to get back to Jesus's ways. To do that, let's look at the example of multiplication that Jesus gave in Mark 4.

Practice Activity:

Take a minute to read Mark 4:1-19 and answer the questions below.

1. What does the story tell us about the kingdom of God?

2. What did you like about the story?

3. What does good soil look like?

4. How do you find or identify good soil?

5. Which soil describes where you are today?

6. What do you need to remove from the soil of your life?

7. What does the story tell us about God, discipleship, and kingdom vision?

8. Which soil do you want to be?

13

Before diving into this chunk of scripture, let's take a brief detour. Ask yourself if you think you could lead a group by reading Scripture (or telling the story) and then asking those simple questions? Hopefully your answer is yes! Everybody should be able to do that because it's simple and reproducible.

Those are what we call Discovery Questions that can be used in groups in cultures all over the world. Using this method teaches the group that the Holy Spirit is the teacher, not some dynamic person. It teaches them that the body of Christ is about participating not spectating, and it is highly beneficial for churches to start off that way. Whether you are reading this by yourself or participating in a group study, the point in this exercise is to see something simple and reproducible.

If you completed the exercise, you're already doing the stuff we've introduced in this chapter! Likely, you will have something you feel like the Holy Spirit taught you through it that you could share with someone.

Below are some examples of responses we've received from other trainings.

- Truth is only given through revelation of the Holy Spirit to those who pursue Him for it.

- God's running a till through our soil. There's some good soil, some bad soil, there's some manure, and there's all that stuff; but as we let him use us, that tiller takes all the bad stuff and mixes it all in to where it's nothing but good. It makes it good, usable soil.

- Soil does not necessarily start off good, but should be worked to the point of becoming fruit-bearing soil. Hard ground must be broken up. Stones and thorns need to be removed.

- Many hesitate to "witness" for fear of rejection; however, the believer's only responsibility is to sow the seed, not determine the result.

Searching for Good Soil

I love that last response! It is a profound statement because it takes the pressure off us. It's our responsibility to share, and we're certainly looking for good soil; but the only way we know who has good soil is by their response. Good soil will receive, and then they will grow and reproduce over and over again.

This idea of searching out the good soil is very important. For the sake of emphasis, let's break this passage of Scripture into four even parts according to the four different types of soil. It seems to be that three-quarters of the different soils don't reproduce like good soil should reproduce. This is very important to keep in mind as it is easy to get discouraged when people don't respond. There is going to be a larger number of people who don't respond; but there are, in fact, people out there that will respond, so we must not give up. There is good soil out there.

Don't forget, God will use us to help (cultivate) bad soil as well. He can and will use us to break up the ground, remove rocks, and thorns. Discipleship is a process of cultivating and nourishing good soil in our lives and others. It's hard work!

"Let us not become weary in doing good, at the proper time we will reap a harvest if we do not give up." ~Galatians 6:9

The Story of all Stories

We will discuss a Person of Peace in more detail in the next chapter, but this is someone through whom we may find more good soil. One of the things I love about this story in Mark 4 is that Jesus described it as the story of all stories.

He basically told the disciples that if they didn't grasp this story on multiplication and His kingdom, they wouldn't understand any of His stories. That statement is found in Mark 4:13 and is very interesting. If we don't understand this story, how can we understand any of His stories? How can we understand His Kingdom?

If this is the parable of all parables, and it is a Kingdom vision that Jesus is giving His disciples on multiplication, then we need to be sowing seeds broadly and looking for good soil. What you and I can tend to do is pick out where we sow the seeds. Remember King Saul? How he was handsome, and head and shoulders above all the other men? We have a tendency to gravitate toward that person, and predetermine for ourselves if they are the kind of person that is going to be good soil.

I've heard missionary trainers say that we just need to go and choose disciples, but I've learned that is not the most effective way to go. I would end up choosing Judas every time. Out of the 12 disciples, he's the most educated, has the most money, looks the best, and isn't a poor fisherman or tax collector or thief. He seems to be the guy that has it all together, and I'll choose him every time.

Instead, if we let the Holy Spirit choose by giving people the Word of God, the good soil will be revealed by whether they are faithful and obedient. We have to allow God to choose them, and when we see where God is at work, then we join Him.

Seeing where God is at work starts with some good engagement strategies. An engagement strategy is basically a way we can develop relationships to find those who are receptive or good soil.

In our network, we use several ways to test the soil of people's hearts. These tools help us discern where God is at work. Learning to ask good questions is very helpful. For example:

"Is there a miracle you need from God and can I pray for you about it?"

"How can I pray for you?"

"Are you near to or far from God?"

"Can I tell you a story or show you a picture of how God changed my life?"

Practice in asking good questions, sharing your story, and transitioning to sharing His Story is key in finding good soil. Again, when we are in relationship with people we are also engaged in the cultivation process that is helping to develop good soil.

Give it Away

It is our hope that you will take the things you read in this book, and share them with someone else.

As we have mentioned, our vision is to multiply and reproduce disciple-making disciples through the principles being taught. Everything given is meant to be shared with someone else. The whole point is to give it away. The job and role of the teacher and equipper is to teach others to teach.

As a matter of fact, 2 Timothy 4:3 says this:

"For the time, will come when people will not put up with sound doctrine. Instead, to suit their own desires, they will gather around them a great number of teachers to say what their itching ears want to hear."

Those teachers will only be looking to gather listeners, which will lead to the development of a host-parasite relationship. We want to see the opposite. We want to challenge people to go and do what they've been told to do.

Our desire is for everyone to share everything we are teaching with someone else. This chapter has already provided some vision casting stories and tools, and more will be provided throughout the remainder of the book. Will you be obedient to use them? Will you be a doer of the word and not just a hearer?[5]

Testimony

In 2014, I took an 11-month journey overseas. It took some time to regroup after such a journey; but about five months after returning, and as a result of the transformation that has been occurring in my life, I felt as though I was given the gift of a fresh perspective. I was a part of the original suburban house church where the M4 Network was birthed. However, over the years, I believe I lost sight of the vision because of the ways I was bound spiritually and the box I kept God in. The vision of the M4 Network is not about the Network; rather it is a combining and uniting of efforts to bring the Kingdom of God to all people.

Though updates are regularly sent, I still failed to recognize just how much the Network had expanded beyond our house church gathering and the significance of the need to pursue more than just a healthy functioning weekly meeting. That is important, but it is only a piece. Recently, I attended a vision casting meeting where I was reminded of the intent of the Network. I have also had the privilege of being more exposed to the ways God is granting Guy and other members of the Network favor and ripe harvest fields.

The M4 Network was formed for the sole purpose of expanding God's Kingdom by training disciples to train disciples to train disciples; so that as they meet, a church is formed and then multiplied as they continue the process.

---

[5] James 1:22

This is happening in multiple prison units. Men, who were trained by Guy or other M4 partners, were leading within the prison; and now are being released, and training and leading in the city. This is happening through connections that are being made across various states where people are coming to receive training through the Network in order to carry out these principles in their communities. This work is being carried out all across Houston and the outlying areas, as well as in other cities, states, and countries. It was exciting to recently sit in the company of men representing all these different areas, encouraging and teaching one another in the principles, and celebrating together all that God is doing.

- Kristin Funderburg, M4 Network

Chapter 2
Where do We go?
(Ministry)

The idea of Living Out Reproducible Discipleship contains some basic principles which will be addressed throughout this chapter. The first question we want to ask regarding making disciples is: "Where are we supposed to go to make disciples?" Then, along with the principles, we will provide some practical methods and tools to help you engage in conversations.

Go Solo vs. Two by Two

Each of us has a responsibility to start with engaging our family and friends. This is a place where it is usually safe to go by ourselves, or solo. The first principle is to learn how to effectively share our story. Toward the end of this chapter, we will provide a simple tool and tips to help develop your story.

Once we learn to effectively share our story, we need to learn how to use it as a bridge to share God's story. Throughout the Gospels we see various examples of where people go to share their stories.

One guy, for example, wanted to travel with Jesus, but he was told to stay right where he was and tell his story to the people he knew. Another time, Jesus sent multiple guys into an unreached town to find pockets of people, and to find a person of peace within those pockets. From these two examples, we see this principle where we can go solo to family and friends, but go with at least two people into a new area. There's a great story that shows us why it is so important to go by two's when you go to a new pocket of people.

Some of the partners that I work with were training young men to travel to Chinese villages. They went to start a new business with the intention of using business to share the gospel. This village was so impoverished that the village elders began to bring their daughters to these young businessmen. The elders were asking the men to take their daughters as mistresses because they believed the men could offer them a better life and in turn help their families.

Since these guys went by two's, they were able to encourage one another and stay accountable to not take the girls. Imagine if they had sent one guy by himself. The temptation would have been overwhelming with these fathers basically throwing their daughters at them out of desperation.

That story provides just one reason why accountability is needed when going to new areas or pockets of people. I work with some guys that go into sports bars, and we say to never leave a guy alone in one of the sports bars. We always go in with at least two.

Another reason to intentionally go out with at least two people is that sometimes, both or all people are not necessarily needed for equal participation in the conversation. This leads us to another important principle. Whoever is not doing the talking should be praying. Continual prayer is a simple, practical principle to be intentional about, but very important and powerful.

There is only one example that I'm aware of in the New Testament where someone went to a pocket of people alone, and that is when Paul was in Athens. He was dropped off by a team; and while he was waiting for another team, he decided to wander around the city. As he walked around, he noticed they were a religious culture, and that they had a statue to an "unknown god". He used that statue as a bridge to share the Gospel, and tell them who the unknown god was.

Remember that he was only alone because he was waiting for another team, and he was being faithful while he waited for them. The principles of when to go solo and when to go two by two are important; but there may be times, like what Paul encountered, where the principal is appropriately violated. Don't think we're saying to never share when you're alone, but that these principles are best to follow as often as you can.

One other fascinating story worth mentioning is about a man named Bruce Olsen, who tried to go to South America with a team, but ended up alone for a while. *Bruchko and the Motilone Miracle*[iii] is the powerful sequel to Bruce Olson's best-selling missionary classic, *Bruchko*;[iv] and is a remarkable tale of adventure, tragedy, faith, and love. It shows how, despite incredible dangers and obstacles, one humble man and a tribe of primitive, violent Indians, by joining together in simple obedience, have been transformed forever by the sovereign will of God. This book, which details Olson's missionary work and events from the 1970s to the present, will stir and encourage the hearts of readers to serve and follow God passionately.

We strongly encourage you to first go to your family and friends because that helps train you how to share your faith. Additionally, God has placed these people in your life for a reason. Why would we not make sure we seek out those most closely connected to us first? Even if we are not close to them, God still chose them to be our family; and we should make every effort to at least make sure they have the chance to hear what God has done for us. So, before we send missionaries across cultures, we first start teaching and training them among their family and friends.

Personally, I will not affirm and support someone as a cross-cultural missionary if they haven't led anyone to Christ in their own culture. It's funny how we can be so quick to go to other cultures, and then start realizing we haven't even prayed about people coming to Christ in our own culture.

You know there are people all around us who don't know Christ. Why aren't we intentional to share when we're here, wherever "here" may be? That's the whole point. We need to be faithful here and there, and here is our training ground of faithfulness.

Jesus says, "If you're faithful in little, I will make you faithful in much."[6]

The Person of Peace

In Mark 5, we find the story from the example above about a guy who was full of legions of demons, and was healed by Jesus. The newly healed man wanted to follow wherever Jesus was going, but Jesus instructed him to go back to his home and share what happened.

When he goes and shares his story with those he knows, they can see the change in him, but he doesn't stop there. He continues throughout the Decapolis;[7] and the combination of him sharing His story, and having a truly transformed life, leaves them in awe of God. It is so powerful that 10 cities were transformed by the good news of Jesus Christ.

That guy is what we call a person of peace. He is a bridge person through which the gospel flowed to all these other people. In Luke 10, when we see Jesus sending the disciples out in multiple teams of two, He is sending them out to find a person

---

[6] Matthew 25:23
[7] 10 cities that span around 70 miles

24

of peace. He tells them to go into the home of the town where they are sent, and say to the home, "The peace of God is on you." If they are receptive, He said to stay there a while, proclaim the kingdom of God, heal, and do the things that He has been teaching and empowering them to do.

Let's use Luke 10 to identify the principles of finding a person of peace. Jesus sent them out in two's, and said they should go to a household. The Greek word for household is a word called 'oikos', and that doesn't really mean just one family.

In the East, a household is full of people. It's full of servants. It's full of extended family, even up to four generations. It is a household of a network of relationships. When I go to Ethiopia, the upper-middle class homes usually house at a minimum a guard, gardener, a cook, and extended family.

The household is full of people. So when Jesus said to go to a home, He was talking about going to an oikos, or a network of various relationships among the people inside. Then He said to speak peace to it and if they are receptive, follow the receptivity.

There are three R's that can help us remember what to look for when we are searching for a person of peace. When people receive us as representatives and ambassadors of God's Kingdom it is the same as them receiving the Kingdom. Receptivity is one of the keys to community transformation.

The first thing we want to look for then, in a person of peace, is someone who is *Receptive*. Remember, in the last chapter, we talked about different soils, and that we should look for good soil to really invest in. Good soil will look like someone who is receptive or a person of peace.

Secondly, we want to look for a person who has a *Reputation*, and the reputation can be either good or bad. People feared the demonized guy in Mark 5 who lived among the tombs and no one could subdue him, until Jesus approached him. Although his reputation was bad, a lot of people knew about him.

Finally, the third thing is that a person of peace will have *Relational Connections*. They are people who are connected to a lot of others. When we look in the Gospels and in the book of Acts, there are tons of examples of people who meet these criteria for a person of peace.

One great example is a man named Cornelius. His story is found in Acts 10, when the Gospel first goes to the Gentiles. He has a good reputation; and is known as a good soldier, who fears God, and does good things. God sends an angel to tell Cornelius to send for a man named Peter in a nearby town. Simultaneously, God gives Peter a vision to reveal that he has had the wrong perspective about the extent of the Gospel.

In the vision, a sheet comes down containing food that Peter has considered unclean, but God is telling him that he needs to learn to thank Him for all food. God is not just referring to food here, but is preparing Peter to learn to relate to the Gentiles.

In the vision, God tells Peter to go meet Cornelius. Peter obediently goes, and finds Cornelius to be very receptive. Because of his influence, Cornelius's entire household, or oikos, shows up receptive as well. So, he has become a bridge for all of these other people, his network of relationships, to come to Christ.

We see this over and repeatedly as a strategy of Jesus and the apostles. Jesus started the process in Luke 10 with the disciples; and then we see Paul and the apostles following the same process throughout the Scriptures. More examples are provided following the next few paragraphs that will allow us to explore Scripture a little more on this topic.

We said that we need to find people who are receptive, who have reputation, and who have relational connectedness; however, we end up taking people out of and away from their network and relationships to teach or train them. While there may be times someone truly needs to be removed from an environment, we don't want to make that a regular practice.

We want to help people learn how to be obedient right where they are, and reach the people they are connected to.

Practice Activity:

Take some time to look through the examples listed below of people of peace that can be found in Scripture. Then, try to think of some other examples in Scripture where someone went by themselves to share with family and friends and had some come to Christ. Think through any other examples of people of peace, whether good or bad reputation.

Examples:

- Cornelius – Acts 10:1-33

- Lydia – Acts 16:11-15, 40

- Philippian Jailer - Acts 16:25-34

- Jason - Acts 17:1-9

- Woman at the Well – John 4:1-42

- The guy with legion of demons – Mark 5:1-20

- The blind man - John 9:1-41

- Crispus - Acts 18:7-8

Our hope is that you can see that there are so many examples throughout scripture that support the idea of finding a person of peace. Unfortunately, most churches in America think that they can simply put out a sign; and say, "Come grow with us!" in order to reach the world.

It's important to note that in the 1950's in the U.S., 99% percent of the people invited to a church gathering would accept the invitation. The George Barna Group and other researchers are saying that now only 40% will respond to an invitation in the most receptive areas. In some areas it could be as low as 15%. If this is true, what does this say about only using an attractional approach to our mission?

There is research out that says this is not true, but the issue is a lack of discipleship and invitation by those who are church members.[8]

"Come grow with us?" That may be brutally honest, but that's commonly what we do. We think good marketing plans are really going to make it all happen. Now, God can use some of that. I'm not saying, He can't or doesn't use it; but I'm asking why we don't follow the principles and the patterns that Jesus and the apostles demonstrated?

I'm telling you, the person of peace is a pattern that is seen throughout Scripture, but we don't think like that because we are church program-minded and not missionary-minded. We need to be missionary-minded as disciples of Christ if we want to see the gospel multiplied.

One of the problems is that we don't read the Bible for ourselves. We think the professionals should tell us their opinion and insight. We continue drinking milk, and wanting someone

---

[8] Below are some resources containing this research.
Growing Your Church From the Outside In by George Barna
https://www.barna.com/research/five-trends-among-the-unchurched/
http://factsandtrends.net/2013/09/13/church-attendance-remains-steady/#.V_kCdOArKhc

else to talk to us about the Bible; rather than eating solid meat, which is learning to read the Bible ourselves.

The main thing is to walk away from all of this asking, "What can I do personally?" and "How can I teach someone else to do the same thing?" We must start with learning to share our story; and when someone first comes to Christ, teach and encourage them to share their story.

Learning to Share Your Story

It should be easy to share our story, and teach someone how to share their story. Sometimes we can over complicate things, but anyone should be able to begin practicing this on the spot using the tool below.

Learning how to share our story can be broken into three sections.

- What was my life like before Christ?

- How did I come to know Christ?

- How is my life different since knowing Christ?

Some people may have testimonies that have a longer "before Christ" story than others, and may need to do more summarizing in that section. So, for the first section, a simple summary could be something like, "I was involved in drugs." or "I lied a lot." Focus on the things that you may have done to fulfill areas of your life where you felt empty. Maybe you were depressed or sad or miserable or selfish.

In the second section, you will explain how you came to know Christ. Be clear in explaining how you know that you have eternal life so your listener knows that they can have eternal life too. Did you have an extreme life event or something that pushed you closer to him (i.e. an accident, etc.)? Or has it been a process of understanding and realization over time?

Finally, for the third section, you will explain how your life is different since you came to know Christ. Maybe your life is more fulfilling. Maybe you have a better sense of purpose now. If Jesus has truly transformed you, then you will likely not have that long list of struggles now that you had in that "Before Christ" section. You might be a better mother or a better father.

A few more tips to keep in mind would be to avoid using "churchy" words. Not everyone truly understands the meaning of words like salvation, sanctification, righteousness, etc. Remember that we should be sharing our story with the love of Christ. We don't want to just try to sound good or get through a speech.[9] Be careful to ensure they are engaged and following you. Know your audience by having a real conversation. Ask questions, and listen to where they came from and where they are.

Another good idea is to learn how to lengthen or shorten your story based on the opportunity. It helps to have in mind a 30 second version, a three-minute version, and a 10-15 min version. We have provided a tool in the appendices[10] to help you learn how to break down your story in order to hit the main points and summarize.

Story Examples

Ryan Orbin, M4 Network

Thirty-two months ago I was on my knees in a white paper suit in the holding tank of the Harris County Jail crying out to God for the first time in my life. I had just spent the past 24 hours in a pure psychosis state,

---

[9] 1 Corinthians 2:1-2
[10] Appendix A: My Story

running through the streets, believing that I was being chased by people who weren't really there. I had stolen two cars in that time period, trashed a motel room and was tasered by the police. After trying to run again, they stripped me of my clothes and took me to the jail.

It was at this moment, after seventeen years of meth addiction, that I finally realized I needed a Savior. I cried out to God and repented – "turned and followed!". Over the next three weeks in jail, Jesus began to show Himself to me in such real ways that I wouldn't even believe if I hadn't experienced them myself. I had an experience very much similar to Paul on the road to Damascus, or maybe it was more like Nebuchadnezzar when he lost his mind. Whatever the case, the change that Jesus has done in my life has been very dramatic, and all in just over two and a half years.

JC Sandoval, M4 Network

My name is JC and I'm from Houston, TX. I'm nineteen years old, and I was raised in a neighborhood where the things you knew only came from what you happened to see. As I got closer to Christ, I saw more things working all around me. Growing up, from the ages three to sixteen, I had witnessed and went through so much that I just started thinking more about my life. It was so common in my neighborhood to see drug dealing, violence, pistols being carried, and most of all gangs getting into it with other gangs.

So now that I'm one of the few who made it out of the neighborhood I was in, I go back into the hoods of Houston to serve. I don't go just to serve, but to share the gospel. With the things I now know, I'm able to go back and be a helping hand to others who are in the position I used to be in. I gave my life to Christ when I was sixteen years old, and He has made me a better man. I'm so thankful God has worked through amazing people to help me grow.

Practice Activity:

Write out bullet points for each section as detailed above, and practice sharing a three-minute version of your story.

The Challenge

Once you have practiced sharing your story, begin to list the names of people that you know need to hear it. Who do you know that needs to come to know Christ or is far from God?

We tend to find that people who have been in church for a while struggle to come up with any names. If that is your situation, then you need to pray about places to go to find and connect with people who are far from God.

Below is a list of scriptures with blanks in them.[11] You can fill in those blanks with the names that you have listed and pray for them. It is important to learn to pray God's Word because true movements start with the practice of prayer.

Strategic Prayer Focus[v]

- Lord, I pray that you draw _____ to Yourself. **(John 6:44)**

- I pray that _____ would seek to know You. **(Acts 17:27)**

- I pray that _____ would hear and believe the Word of God for what it really is. **(1 Thessalonians 2:13)**

- I ask You, Lord, to prevent Satan from blinding _____ to the truth. **(2 Cor. 4:4; 2 Tim. 2:25-26)**

---

[11] Appendix B: Strategic Prayer Focus

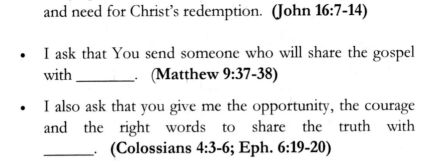

- Holy Spirit, I ask you to convict _____ of his/her sin and need for Christ's redemption. **(John 16:7-14)**

- I ask that You send someone who will share the gospel with _____. **(Matthew 9:37-38)**

- I also ask that you give me the opportunity, the courage and the right words to share the truth with _____. **(Colossians 4:3-6; Eph. 6:19-20)**

- Lord, I pray that _____ would turn from his/her sin and follow Christ. **(Acts 17:30-31; 2 Thessalonians 1:9; 10)**

- Lord, I pray that _____ would put all of his/her trust in Christ. **(John 1:12, 5:24)**

- Lord, I pray that _____ would confess Christ as Lord, take root and grow in faith, and bear much fruit for Your glory. **(Rom. 10:9-10; Col. 2:6-7; Luke 8:15)**

One of the ways we want to challenge you is to commit to pray over this list daily. Something that helps me remember to pray for my list is to set my phone alarm for 10:02 AM or 10:02 PM.

Neil Cole was the first to introduce me to this. The idea comes from Luke 10:2, where Jesus says, "The harvest is plentiful, but the workers are few. Ask the Lord of the harvest, therefore, to send out workers into his harvest field". He sends the disciples, and sends us, out of the fold and into the fields, as lambs among wolves, where we are desperate for a shepherd. He sends us because the lost sheep are out in the fields; and as we go out and seek them, we must walk in desperate dependence on the Shepherd. Setting an alarm for 10:02 is helpful because it leads us back to Scripture as the reminder to pray over our lists. There are many within the M4 Network, as well as partnering networks

33

who do this, so you will be joining a large number in begging God to move through our personal networks.

In John 4, Jesus pulls His disciples aside. After sharing with a woman, that His culture said He should not have been talking to, and after going to a place that He should not have been going to; He says, "Guys, open your eyes, the field is white with harvest." This simply means that there are receptive people all around us. We just need our eyes opened. May this be your prayer, "Lord, open my eyes to see those who need Your love and Your life."

There are two pieces to the challenge that was just presented, and we want to invite you to commit to them and participate. First, make your list and pray regularly over it; and second, commit to share your story with someone in the next two weeks.

Setting a goal is a good way to push us to carry out commitments. I typically challenge people to share with five people, and that is usually a good goal. Take some time to pray and intentionally look for five people to share your story with over the next couple of weeks.

It may help to share and do this with someone, so that you can keep each other accountable to do it. If you went through the exercise earlier, you have already shared your story with believers; and now we want to encourage you to share it with someone who does not know Christ. Even just looking for opportunities is a good place to start.

Note for those doing work in large cities:

I would like to address those looking for people of peace in an urban/suburban setting. We need to be aware of the complexities that are involved in large cities. When someone moves into an urban area, they usually struggle with isolation even though they are surrounded by millions of people, and this affects their oikos or network of relationships. This creates a little more difficulty in urban settings to reach larger groups of people because of its complexities and isolation. Usually what you will find is receptive individuals, or 2 or 3 who are willing to meet for discipleship.

This makes it hard to get to movement. However, that being said, there are certain tribes or affinity groups that serve as network hubs that help us connect people more effectively in urban settings.

We have found this to be true with Hip Hop culture in Houston. People who connect with us feel like they are part of a tribe, a community, and a sense of belonging is developed. We do use events with intent. The Hip Hop Hope events help us mine networks of relationships in communities and helps connect people to a "tribe" of belonging.

We are trying to implement this strategy among other tribes or affinity groups. Using select sports would be another example.

In large cities, we need team strategies and having a critical mass or larger community to connect with has some validity. Individuals will tend to reach individuals, but teams will reach more people and help catalyze movement in the big city.

In rural movements, when you identify people of peace (key leaders) you are practically guaranteed a large number of people will follow when they follow. This is not true in most large cities. People are just far more isolated; and the sociological structures are radically different, with lots of complexities.

While we need to be aware that rural and urban outreach strategies are two different cats, we still must get people to start sharing the Gospel with their family and friends and utilizing a tool called a ministry map (discussed in Chapter 4). There is more than one way to skin a cat, and that certainly applies to big cities.

Stories From the Field

How have you built relationships with unreached people? Where do you go?

By simply going into those dark places and relating to them and what they're doing, still continuing to be the light. For example, I've been to an apartment where they were smoking weed and drinking beer, but I still spoke to them about Jesus and how He loved them no matter where they were. I didn't judge them on what they were doing. No matter how comfortable I am in my faith, I never judge. I just told them about Jesus and how much Jesus loves them. Also, I've been to a bar/pool hall and was able to pray for people there. So, just basically relating to them right there where they are. Just loving them and not wanting to make them feel like they have to change up or switch up just to talk to you.

- Karen Bogdanyi, M4 Network

All kinds of ways, whether it's through my car, my clothes, by not being judgmental. The biggest one is loving somebody right where they're at. That's my biggest tool – love them right where they're at and work on me all the time. That keeps me at a friend basis in order for me to be there when they really, really wanna reach out for God.

- Disciple The Streets, M4 Network

Chapter 3
What Do We Say and Do?
(Message)

In this chapter, we want to address how you can sit down with someone and go through the Gospels or some stories of Christ to help them discover who Christ is. This is a very simple way to begin the discipleship process early in someone's life. We'll talk about why it's important, and its effectiveness.

Know Your Audience

As we initiate a relationship with someone we think is receptive to the gospel and discipleship, it is very important to be a good listener. Listening shows them we care, and it allows them to share their story. Have you ever met someone, and all they did was talk? Or do you maybe even have some current relationships where all they do is talk? How does that make you feel? Like they don't care much about what you have to say, right? Or all they want to hear about is their self? If you're honest, you might even admit that you feel like they're somewhat selfish and self-centered.

Creating situations where we do most of the talking may incidentally be communicating that our only agenda is to present something rather than engage in genuine conversation. That is a problem. Do we really expect people to respond to an invitation to a personal relationship with Jesus if we don't show that we care about where they are or how they've reached the point they're at?

On the flip side of that, we have to be careful not to let the relationship itself become a god. There have been a lot of teachings on relational evangelism; but unfortunately, people often end up focusing too much on the relationship, and then become afraid to share the gospel for fear of losing the relationship. We must be careful to not place more value on a relationship than on introducing them to God. We want to love people, and we want to share the love of God with them.

We just learned how to share our story at the end of the last chapter. One of the best ways to move toward sharing our story is by listening to someone and asking them to share their story with us. Asking someone to share their story first allows us to adapt our story to better communicate the gospel message that will meet them right where they are.

We've all heard it said that love is a verb. If so, then we need to demonstrate our love with action. As a network, some of the ways we demonstrate that we care about people is by giving backpacks and school supplies, helping clothe people, and meeting needs in whatever way we can. We need to consider the intangible needs by asking people where they're hurting or struggling. There are needs everywhere we go.

It is important to always be ready, willing, and able to share your story and His story. It can be as simple as, "God has changed me. He can change you, and He desires to change the world. That's the incredible good news!" That statement is a simplified example of the principle of going from "My story" to "His story".

A Reproducing Cycle

Let's look at how these principles become a reproductive cycle. We start by engaging people and sharing our story, and then we bridge to His story - the Gospel. As we move forward, we will begin to see the principles moving in a circular motion.

Remember the discussion in the first chapter about having a big enough vision to think small. There is a holistic reproductive cycle, but it consists of smaller steps which must frequently be reproduced in order to see movement. *(See graphic on the front cover.)*

After we've shared His story, we start talking about making and multiplying disciples. When groups of disciples start gathering together, churches form; and the cycle continues reproducing. The principles that follow sharing "His Story" will be covered in the coming chapters, but we want to give you a quick glimpse of the whole picture to help cast vision for repeating the cycle.

If we want to see disciples reproduce, we must start from the very beginning. This can be looked at in three steps. First, we learn to engage people and share our story. Second, we learn to share His story, the Gospel. Then we learn how to combine those, and share our story as a bridge to His story. It is important that we don't stop there. When a person receives the Gospel presentation, it is important to immediately teach them these things, and urge them to begin sharing it. We help someone grow by modeling how the life of a disciple should look, and teaching them how a disciple is made. If you were to ask a group of believers in America to explain what a disciple is, the likely response would be that they are a follower. However, if we were to search scripture, we would find that Jesus's definition is so much more descriptive. Some of the things He said are pretty amazing!

To pique your interest, here are a few examples of the characteristics of a disciple that we find from Jesus. A disciple is:

- willing to surrender their life

- willing to give of themselves

- willing to lay down their life and pick up their cross

- willing to die daily

- committed to sharing the gospel with others

- committed to making disciples who make disciples

There are so many times where Jesus said, "If you don't, then you cannot be My disciple";[12] but we tend to avoid those things. These are known as conditional "If-then" statements. Again, this is where we will tip toe around trying not to offend people, or we ourselves struggle with being willing to really commit wholeheartedly. Jesus even said that those who are not offended by Him are blessed.[13]

Since Jesus shows us that being a disciple is much more than just being a follower, we are focused on going through this reproductive process. To reproduce means to multiply or to increase, so we're going to be talking about how to make more and more disciples.

Milk vs Meat

Let's keep in mind our initial vision for multiplication. We've looked a lot at our mindset and how most churches train us to think addition. I want us to look at some verses in Hebrews 5 that relate to multiplying disciples and maturity in our lives.

"We have much to say about this, but it is hard to make it clear to you because you no longer try to understand. In fact, though by this time you ought to be teachers, you need someone to teach you the elementary truths of God's word all over again. You need milk, not solid food! Anyone who lives on milk, being still an infant, is not acquainted with the teaching about

---

[12] John 8:1-32
[13] Matthew 11:6

righteousness. But solid food is for the mature, who by constant use have trained themselves to distinguish good from evil."

Hebrews 5:11-14 (NIV)

The author is saying here that they ought to be teachers by now. This is why we've been talking about teachers having the job of teaching others to teach, and not just gather listeners.

Teach others to teach others.

He continues to confront them that not only are they not doing this; but it's almost like they've forgotten that they should, and are slow to learn. Something has happened, and then he goes into an example about how they are still drinking milk.

Now, I've already mentioned many times that I go to Africa a lot. If I sit with a bunch of Africans, and ask them where milk comes from, their answers will be different than most Americans. We might guess that their answer would be cows, and most Americans would likely say the grocery store; but many Africans would actually say it comes from their mother.

I've had tons of different meetings while in Africa. Sometimes they're underground, which simply means that it's a secret meeting due to persecution of those in the faith; and sometimes we have the privilege of meeting above ground. Regardless of the environment, many of the mothers openly nurse in the same room. They don't have formula. They don't have stores to go to. In many of the places that I work, milk comes from mama.

This is important because we, in America, will think differently than that. Thinking back to the Hebrews 5 passage, the author is confronting his audience that they are still having to go to a secondary source to be fed rather than learning how to feed themselves. Therefore, they are slow to learn. The culture that seems to rule here in our western world is to look at a teacher or pastor, and say, "Pastor/Teacher, the problem here is that you're just teaching me milk. If you would teach me some meat…" We put the problem off on the pastor or teacher. We interpret this passage as though it is somebody else's responsibility to teach us some deep stuff.

On the contrary, the message communicated in this passage is that we need to learn how to feed ourselves. I remember seeing the movie Grown Ups,[vi] with Adam Sandler, that shows a highly disturbing image. He, his buddies, and their wives are sitting around talking and the wife of one of his buddies was still breastfeeding their five-year-old. I'm certainly not promoting this as a positive family movie, but this example had me grossly disturbed. Something is not right about that! In the same way, the author of Hebrews is telling us that there is something not right about us still going to someone else to be our teachers, rather than us learning how to feed ourselves and teach others.

Our ultimate responsibility as Christ followers, in making disciples, is to teach them to teach others. All of this starts with learning to feed ourselves. Unfortunately, what happens more frequently is that people are won to church with programs and events, but are never won to Christ and His Word. Though this is not always true, there is a need to seriously evaluate the idea that what you win them with, you likely win them to.

My own story is that I came to Christ reading God's word, and I can tell the difference that it made in my life. There was a man at Metropolitan Baptist Church that took me in. He saw something in me, being 20 years old, and he told me he wanted to spend some time with me. I gladly accepted; and as he began to meet with me, he said, "Man, you have an incredible understanding of this stuff!"

He asked how I got involved and connected with the church, so I shared that I had come to Christ in my bedroom, reading the New Testament. I had read it through about three or four times before I met this guy; and he took notice of the difference in my life, which was all because I started out reading God's Word.

Rather than expecting a pastor or teacher to tell me what to believe, I had received teaching from the Spirit of God. I'm not saying we don't need teachers or that God hasn't used teachers to help me. There were a lot of things that I was off-base with. What I am saying is that we need to start teaching people to teach others how to feed themselves.

Discovery is Key

The key point we want to communicate is that the best way to lead someone to Christ is to lead them directly to the Scriptures, where they can read and see and discover God for themselves. One way to do this with someone is what we call a Discovery Study[vii]. Once we share our story and His story, one of the best things to do is sit down with someone and go through one of the Gospels with them. It's also good to consider taking them through a specific story set[14] leading them through miracles, promises, and commands of Jesus. We want the new disciple to know what it means to be the church, and function that way A.S.A.P.!

As we read through Scripture with someone, we want to be sure not to spend the whole time talking, but allow them to discover by us asking them questions. These questions are simple and can be used with any story.

Discovery Study Questions:

---

[14] Appendix C: Stories of Hope

- What did you like?

- What did you learn about God?

- What did you learn about people?

- What would you change after reading the story?

- Who do you want to share with something that you learned today?

As a reminder, everything provided in this book is intended for you to use and pass on to someone else. We'll talk more about Discovery Studies in a later chapter; but simply put, a discovery study helps us walk someone through the Scripture using simple discovery questions.

We have seen God use this principle of taking somebody through scripture with those five basic questions from here all the way to northern Africa and the Middle East. These studies have been tested, and God has used them over and over. They work because we're teaching them to feed themselves on God's Word and teach others. God's word is living and active and sharper than any two-edged sword.[15]

I used to meet with a guy every Tuesday night that came to Christ this very way. Within the first year of him following Christ, it was unbelievable to sit with him and see the things that God has shown him by just going to the Word. Today, he teaches others in the same way I taught him.

Additionally, the guys that I have discipled in this way don't flinch at reading 20 to 30 chapters per week. When I offer training sessions with people who have been in church for a long time; and tell them we're going to read 20 or 30 chapters, their jaws drop. They think that 20 or 30 chapters per week is too much to

---

[15] Hebrews 4:12

handle. It's not really a lot, but many freak out about it because they're used to only hearing chunks of scripture used in sermons or devotionals.

There are countless times I have tried to encourage people to utilize their Sunday school classes for these Life Change Groups (LCG) and Discovery Studies, but they just can't do it because they can't commit to read. Now, I don't always start out by asking someone to read 20 or 30 chapters. Initially, I may just use a story per week, or a chapter or two that I'll ask them to read over and over again; and then we discuss it when we meet again. I just want to be clear that I'm simply communicating that when someone comes to Christ just by reading God's word, they have a greater hunger and an appetite for reading God's word.

We will make more effective disciples if we will lead them to discover who Jesus is, and why it matters, rather than leading them to make a decision. I believe there is far more ownership of the disciple making process when people discover it themselves. However, there are times, like a midwife, we help "birth" or lead someone to a decision. We will discuss this later in relation to sharing the Three Circles Gospel tool.

We have a tendency to make church attenders and churchgoers, rather than making disciples, and I'm just trying to point out some problems with the current system of the majority. If we just have people show up and check off a checklist that they have been to church, gave as they should, go to Sunday school or a class, listen to a sermon and determine if it contained enough meat; we've lost sight of the principles of discipleship given to us by Jesus. And if we've lost sight of that, then we've lost sight of God's vision that all people in every nation would hear about Jesus.

Those things we just listed are not bad in and of themselves, but everything we do as believers should be motivated by a goal to give out all that we're taking in. People are more inclined to share something they experience; therefore, we need to teach people to feed themselves so they experience God's heart for themselves. The LCG and Discovery Groups help create an environment for that to happen.

Practice Activity:

Take a moment to practice doing a Discovery Study. Look at some different examples of people who shared their stories in the New Testament. Read the scripture and answer the discovery questions - provided below as a reminder.

- John 4:1-26, 39-42

- Mark 5:1-20

- Acts 22:1-21

Discovery Study Questions:

- What did you like?

- What did you learn about God?

- What did you learn about people?

- What would you change after reading the story?

- Who do you want to share with something that you learned today?

We want to encourage you to practice these Discovery Studies to help you see that you can facilitate this type of group. Remember that the idea is not just to read this book or meet in a group of fellow believers; but to go out, practice it, and do it.

Testimony

A multiplication movement should be intentional, yet organic because we must go to people and share, but it is God who will birth his church through us. I believe that multiplication happens when churches are birthed and multiplied up to at least four generations.

- Bobby (Tre9) Herring, M4 Network

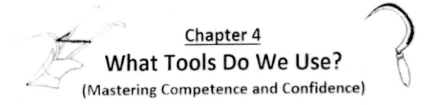

Chapter 4
What Tools Do We Use?
(Mastering Competence and Confidence)

If the ax is dull and its edge unsharpened, more strength is needed, but skill will bring success. Ecclesiastes 10:10 (NIV)

One day, I was invited to go to a L.O.R.D (Living Out Reproducible Discipleship) training and learn simple discipleship tools. It was awesome to see how simple it is to share The Gospel using the Three Circles. At the end of drawing the three circles, I ask them where they are; and based on their answer, I can then ask them where they would want to be. I've used this method since I first learned it, and God has allowed me to lead countless of people to Christ.

- Karen Bogdanyi, M4 Network

If we look at the life of Jesus, which we should always do for our examples, we see that He used a lot of filters. He would use hard sayings[16], parables[17], and the requirement of lordship[18] as filters to determine people's hunger and faithfulness. If we look at the life of most Western Christians, we spend the majority of our time trying to convince people to believe something rather than just sowing seeds and allowing Jesus to show us who is ripe for harvest. Using filters will help us to find where the Lord is working instead of trying to convince someone of something with religion.

---

[16] Matthew 19:16-24; 26:26-28
[17] Mark 4:3-9
[18] Luke 9:23-24

Another common issue we have seen in American Christianity is that there is a lot of assumption. Biblical principles and commands are communicated without providing the tools to carry them out. Typically, in church life we receive lots of exhortation, but very little demonstration and hands on learning in the field.

In nearly everything else in life, we push practice, practice, practice; but somehow it gets left out in spiritual disciplines. Why is there an expectation that with spiritual things, it's just going to come and we don't have to put forth any training effort?

It is the Holy Spirit who works through us, yes; but He doesn't operate us like puppets. True growth comes through faithful obedience. He moves through our obedience as we go; and if we will practice, we will become more effective at listening and operating in Him instead of ourselves.

There are a lot of different methods, tools, and approaches to share the gospel with people; but we encourage everyone we're training to choose just one tool as their go-to for training in the beginning. Simplicity is key for multiplication. When someone is new to sharing the gospel, or when we're training groups, it can become confusing if you try to introduce multiple tools. As people grow spiritually, there's no doubt they will learn more tools; but we want to start with simplicity. This also serves as a filter. If people will not be obedient with one tool, there is no need to give them more.

The Three Circles

The evangelism tool we have been using as a network, and will demonstrate here, is called the Three Circles. It is so easy that it can be reproduced by even a non-believer on the spot.

When you turn on the news, it is clear to see that we live in a world of **Brokenness** and that Brokenness is reflected in people's lives…

The thing about anything broken is that it doesn't start that way. When **God** first created the world, He had a perfect **Design** in mind. Part of that design was that people were whole and lived in perfect relationship with Him...

We entered this brokenness because of something called **Sin** (living life under our own power) which separated us from that relationship with God...

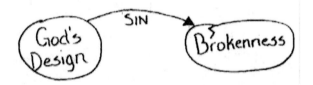

The good news is that God loves us so much that He wanted to give us a way to restore that relationship with Him. That's why He sent His Son, **Jesus**, who lived a perfect life on this earth, and died on the cross to pay for our sins. He was put in a tomb, but didn't stay there. Three days later, He came back to life, and then went back up to Heaven. One day, He will come back for those who are following Him.

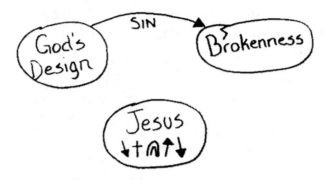

To be reconnected to God, we simply have to do two things. We must **Turn** from our sins and **Follow** Jesus...

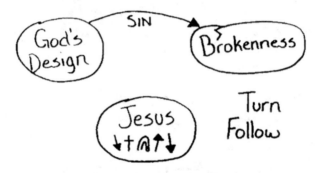

When we do that, Jesus immediately makes us whole again and restores us in relationship with God...

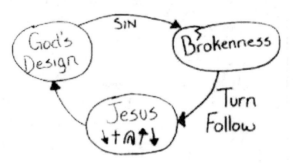

Now, we still live on this earth so we must **Grow** to learn more about God and what it looks like to live for Him; however, He gives us all of Himself and helps us to do that...

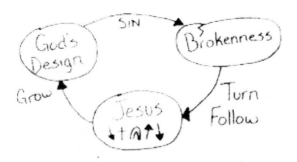

Finally, God's heart is for all people to be made whole, and He commands us to **Go** back into the world of brokenness to share with other people all that He has done for us. That is why I'm here talking to you right now....

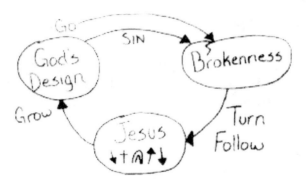

Looking at this, there is really only one of two places you can be. Would you say you are **Near** to or **Far** from God?

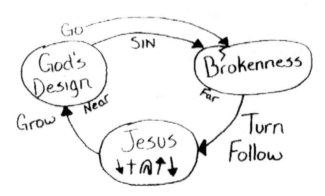

Red Light, Yellow Light, Green Light

As we go out and share the Three Circles, we will encounter three different types of responses from people. These responses are found in Acts 17; and we label them accordingly as a red, yellow, or green light.[19]

"When they heard about the resurrection of the dead, some of them sneered, but others said, 'We want to hear you again on this subject.' At that, Paul left the Council. Some of the people became followers of Paul and believed..." Acts 17:32-34 (NIV)

 RED LIGHT: "... some of them sneered..."

What do we do? We simply lovingly move on. Thank them for their time, but keep it moving. There's no need to try to force or convince anyone. Remember that we are looking for fourth soil![20]

 YELLOW LIGHT: "We want to hear you again on this subject."

What do we do? Once we've shared our story and the Gospel, and see they are not completely uninterested, we ask them if they want to know more. If they say "no", then we know they are a red light and we lovingly move on. But if they say "yes", this is one of the ways a Discovery Study comes into play.

For those who say yes, we immediately ask them for a commitment to take advantage of the door while it is open. "Do

---

[19] Appendix D: F1&F2 Bookmark
[20] Mark 4:8, 20

you want to meet up again to go through some other stories about Jesus and learn more about Him?" Set your next meeting right then and there if they are willing and able. Ask them if they are interested in meeting weekly to keep learning more. This is true whether we are talking with a family member, friend, or complete stranger.

There are four stories of hope[21] that we typically start with when someone is interested in Jesus, but not ready to follow Him right away. If they are truly seeking Jesus, then prayerfully they will come to an understanding of their need for Him. If more than 4 stories are needed, the gospel of John is a great place to continue leading someone through this process. Use the Discovery Study questions as you read each week. Discipleship begins even before someone gives their life to Christ and is more than just talking to somebody one time. It is being willing to walk alongside them as they journey to Christ and ultimately with Him.

When you're bringing someone through a discovery study, you will need to come to a place where you can ask them directly if they are ready to follow Jesus Christ. All you have to do is ask them the question. Jesus was the master question-asker. If you're going to walk through this study with someone, and they begin to see for themselves how amazing this Jesus guy is, you need to know how to lead them to Christ.

GREEN LIGHT: "But some men joined him and believed..."

What do we do? It's important to learn how to tell if someone is open and receptive to Christ, and hopefully the tools

---

[21] The Four Stories of Hope are included under the "Yellow Light" on the bookmark in Appendix D

provided a little further in this chapter can help. A green light may come during an initial encounter with someone; or it may be in the following weeks, months or years of walking them through Discovery Studies in the yellow light process. Therefore, it is extremely important to learn how to help someone understand that there is a necessary step in giving their life to Christ, as well as take them through that process.

Now, this opens some interesting dialogue. A lot of us have heard and been taught something called the "sinner's prayer." There isn't really a "sinner's prayer" in the Bible, but it is okay for us to use it if necessary, and many American Christians have. Personally, I came to Christ by crying out, "Dear God, help me!" I didn't know the sinner's prayer, but that is okay because there is not necessarily a specific "sinner's prayer" that is required. It is a beautiful thing to witness the Holy Spirit at work in someone's heart, so we like to encourage anyone who wants to give their life to Christ to simply express to God what is on their heart.

Again, some people may need to be led in the sinner's prayer. Some people will grow into their faith over time. There are still others who have some sort of cataclysmic event smashed on their head or a crisis that leads them to cry out in faith. Sadly, what we tend to do is say, "My way is the way that everyone needs to come to Christ." But that's not true, right? We all just need to come to Christ.

When someone is interested in learning about the cost of following Christ, our trained believers will meet with them regularly to share biblical truth until a decision to follow or reject Christ is made. For those that reject, we will pray for them and lovingly move on. For those who accept Christ, they will be trained in sharing their faith, sharing the gospel, leading others in discovery studies, plugged into a Body of Christ Gathering, and sent out to repeat the process for others who are far from God. I believe in a simple process with simple tools that anyone can reproduce so that others don't feel intimidated by the pressure of being biblical scholars.

- Bobby (Tre9) Herring, M4 Network

Landing the Plane

We need to learn how to help lead people to Christ. We are emphasizing this because we have seen, many times, that some people are comfortable sharing the Gospel, but don't know what to do to follow through and lead someone to make a decision. So, not only do we need to make sure we know how to share the Gospel, but we also jokingly say we need to know how to land the plane.

Tre9 is the founder of Eyes on Me, Inc. and he and I work closely together. Typically, the hip-hop artists will share the gospel or tell their story at an event, and then ask the audience if they want to respond. In the early years before our L.O.R.D. Trainings, we would ask the Christians volunteering at the event to help us talk through things with the people who were responding, but they would resist because they didn't know what to do.

What would you do in a situation like that?

A good place to start would be to ask them what they came to the altar for. Ask them if they already have Christ in their life. If they say, "No, but I want Him", then you can offer to help lead them if they don't know how or encourage them to just pour their heart out to God. Either way is great; and I've seen some beautiful prayers led by God's Spirit without me leading them, but a lot of people do ask for help. If help is asked for, I'll ask if they mean it and really want it. If they say yes, there are many ways to lead them in a prayer. Remember that there is not a

57

"sinner's prayer" in Scripture. The point is simply a confession of their need for Jesus as their Savior and Lord.

Before we give you a tool to use for leading someone who says they want to give their life to Christ (especially if it is in response to a gospel presentation at an event), in prayer it is good to ask them questions that reveal whether they understand the gospel. Knowing and utilizing the tool taught earlier, the Three Circles, is really helpful here.

Some examples of good questions to ask are:

- Do you believe Jesus died on the cross?

- Do you believe He rose again?

- Do you believe He wants to change your life?

- Do you want Him to change your life?

If they say yes to those questions, then let them know they just need to ask Jesus to do those things. Again, using the Three Circles as a gospel tool is helpful because you have everything you need right in front of you.

We want to provide a simple prayer tool using the Three Circles:

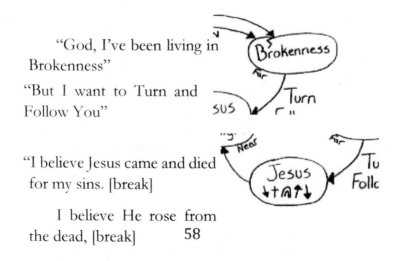

"God, I've been living in Brokenness"

"But I want to Turn and Follow You"

"I believe Jesus came and died for my sins. [break]

I believe He rose from the dead, [break] 58

"Thank You for making me whole again [break]

And allowing me to be in relationship with You

"In Jesus's Name, amen!"

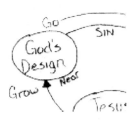

Practice Activity:

Practice leading someone in a simple prayer of confession. You're going to be nervous the first several times if you've never done it before, but that's okay. The only way to become more comfortable is to do it. The more you do it, the more comfortable you'll become little by little. While we need to be prepared to know what to say, ultimately, it's about what the Holy Spirit is doing in that individual through you, so trust Him!

I believe it's kind of like a football game. I never got rid of butterflies, no matter how many times I played. There may always still be a little excitement or nervous energy when we're talking about our faith and helping someone come to Christ. We just need to help guide them, but Jesus does the saving.

Identity

Once someone gives their life to Christ, we are told they immediately gain a new identity based on 2 Corinthians 5:17-21. It is important to lay this foundation for every brand new believer; but also for those who have been walking with Christ and may not have been empowered in their identity.

The process outlined below will help you know how to guide someone through these scriptures to discover their new identity.

First, have the believer (recent or not) read through the entire passage in 2 Corinthians. As with the other tools presented, we want to keep this simple so that it is easily taught and reproduced. Below, we explain everything in detail; however, at the end is a picture with minimal words which is what should be drawn as you are speaking.

"Therefore, if anyone is in Christ, the new creation has come: The old has gone, the new is here! All this is from God, who reconciled us to himself through Christ and gave us the ministry of reconciliation: that God was reconciling the world to himself in Christ, not counting people's sins against them. And he has committed to us the message of reconciliation. We are therefore Christ's ambassadors, as though God were making his appeal through us. We implore you on Christ's behalf: Be reconciled to God. God made him who had no sin to be sin for us, so that in him we might become the righteousness of God."

2 Corinthians 5:17-21 (NIV)

There are two questions we will answer about our identity: "**Who** does it say we are?" and "**How** do we know that?"

Identity
2 Corinthians 5:17-21

Who?

How?

Asking questions gives people a chance to discover the answer themselves instead of just being told. You may start by asking, "Who does it say we are in verse 17?" They should answer "**New Creation**". Take a moment to ensure they understand what that means. Next, ask what else verse 20 says about who we are. The answer here would be "**Ambassador**". Again, take a moment to explain that an ambassador is like a representative.

Identity
2 Corinthians 5:17-21

Who? New Creation & Ambassador

How?

Now, we like to add the analogy that these two aspects of our new identity are like the two sides of a coin. If you look at a quarter (or whatever type of currency is used in your location), it has two different sides, in the U.S., a heads and tails. If you take a quarter with heads on both sides of the coin and try to pay a cashier with it, they will tell you it's fake and not worth 25 cents. Jesus said "Follow me and I will make you fishers of men."[22] We must fish AND follow by being a New Creation AND Ambassador. You can't have one without the other. We will only know our full identity and worth in Christ, when we operate in our full identity.

Explain that you will discuss the Ambassador a little more, but first it is important to know how this is all possible. Have them read verse 21 again, and describe how it is only because of an **Exchange** that took place that allows us to be confident in this identity. Jesus Christ removed our sin entirely by taking our sin on Himself, and placed us in His complete righteousness or made us completely right with God. Our strengths and abilities and good works have nothing to do with us being a new creation and ambassador.

Identity
2 Corinthians 5:17-21

Who? New Creation & Ambassador

How? Exchange

Now, as an ambassador, we need to know where we're going and what we're saying. In verse 18, it tells us that we have a ministry. That ministry is the network of people that are far from God and surround us on a regular basis. Then verse 19 says that we have a message, which is the Gospel. Every believer should

---

[22] Matthew 4:19

be equipped with tools to identify their ministry and know how to share the message.

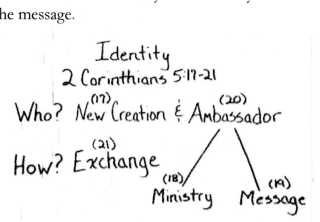

The tool we use to help people identify their ministry is simply called a "Ministry Map" (pictured on the next page). Have the person write their name in the middle of a page and draw a circle around it. Then have them draw out 3-5 lines from that circle, and name at least 3 people (or as many as they can think of) they know who are far from God. Next, have them draw out one or two lines from each of those people, and try to identify someone they might know who is far from God. This can go on as far as they can identify.

For example: Sarah's brother, Josh, is far from God. So, she puts him on her ministry map, and she knows Josh has a friend named Rob who is also far from God. She would put her name in a circle, draw a line and write Josh's name in a circle. She would then draw a line from Josh's name and write Rob in a circle.

Many of us who have been in the Western church for more than two or three years may not as easily identify someone who is far from God because we have been so far removed from those environments. If they don't have a person's name, they can think of places they go regularly or passions they have where they can meet people far from God (i.e. the name of their street, neighborhood, local store, coffee shop, workplace, etc.) We call these People, Places and Passions the 3 P's; and they are a great starting point to begin sharing their story and His Story (the Gospel).

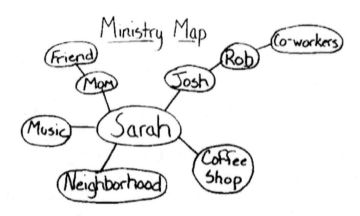

In addition to seeing where to start sharing, we want to encourage people to pray for their Ministry Map daily using the scriptures provided at the end of Chapter Two. This tool is not only a starting point, but helps establish the vision for seeing generations come to Christ and continue reproducing the process of disciple-making disciples.

The tool that our ministry has been teaching for telling the message, the Gospel, is the Three Circles which was just demonstrated in the pages before. It is important to have them learn it right there on the spot so that they know how to communicate the gospel to their loved ones who are far from God. Too often it's seen as necessary to wait for some undetermined amount of time until they're "ready"; but we saw through Practice Activities in the previous chapters already that there was immediate obedience, and even encouragement from Jesus to go share immediately.

Now, we have the full picture of our identity in Christ, according to Scripture, with specific tools to begin obediently living it out.

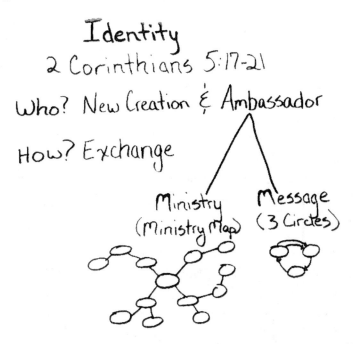

A Testimony by Guy Caskey

Here's a story of a young man, named Anthony, who I used to meet with on Tuesday nights. We went through the book of John together for several months. We moved to Mark, and then when we went to Matthew. He began recognizing that Jesus has been saying the whole time that He is the bread and we should eat of Him. He is saying that He's the water, and we must drink of Him. He is saying that he's the good Shepherd. Jesus is saying that He is the way.

As I watched Anthony put the pieces together, I affirmed how he was seeing that Jesus is saying He is the way. I'm telling you, the whole time he was talking, everything inside of me wanted to put pressure on this guy; but I was aware that God's Spirit was working in his life. I determined that I shouldn't pressure him, but I did need to be willing to ask him a question. After he said that Jesus is all these things, I asked him if he thought he would go to heaven if he were to die that night. Being from a Catholic background, he said yes; but that led me to ask what he would say when he was standing before God and was asked by God why He should let him into His heaven.

Well, Anthony went into describing all the good he had done, and how his good outweighed the bad that he had done. This gave me an opportunity to revisit how we had been going through the gospels for months; and how he had acknowledged that Jesus said that He is the bread of life, He is the way, He is the living water, He is the good Shepherd, etc.

I reminded him how he saw that Jesus said he is the key to everything, and there is no other way that man can be saved. Then I was able to ask him if he was honestly going to stand before God and say that his good outweighed the bad. His mind was blown, and a major light bulb went off. He got it and it was a simple as that. It was like he became born again right in front of my eyes. He said, "I get it. I want to follow Christ." Just by asking some good questions, he came to Christ. I had the privilege of baptizing him and then he baptized his son who came to Christ at his baptism celebration.

Raising Up "Doers"

My vision is to keep things simple, so one of the other illustrations for discipleship that I use is what I like to call, napkin theology. This is a theology that means whatever you are sharing is simple and reproducible enough to fit on a napkin. Sometimes we may use index cards or trifold leaflets that fold into one little page, but the point is the simplicity.

As mentioned at the beginning of this book, what happens in too many teaching scenarios is that we make things so complicated and so in depth, wanting "meat", that we quit teaching people to teach people. In doing that, we build listeners, and Timothy gives us a warning of simply building listeners.

"For the time will come when people will not put up with sound doctrine. Instead, to suit their own desires, they will gather around them a great number of teachers to say what their itching ears want to hear. They will turn their ears away from the truth and turn aside to myths."

2 Timothy 4:3-4 (NIV)

Gathering listeners or listeners gathering teachers is completely opposite of what we should be doing according to what Paul taught Timothy in 2 Timothy 2:2 - to take the things that we are learning and entrust them to faithful ones who will teach others also. We need to keep things simple to better allow this concept of teaching others to tea

Person of Peace

We discussed earlier how to utilize a Discovery Study when you're beginning to share with your family and friends. Now let's look at how it might be a little different when going into a new pocket of people. The first thing we do when going to a new area is to pray our guts out! We should do some research beforehand, and then prayer walk the grounds, being attentive to the things that may reveal the culture.

We're going into an area where it's going to be a little uncomfortable. We will be more aware and intentional about what we do and what we say. There are certain areas in some cities where you wouldn't want to wear certain gang colors. When I go to Ethiopia, I don't want to wear a cross necklace unless I am working strictly with Orthodox people, and then I will wear an Orthodox cross.

In some places, we will use an event with intent. Without intent, we just have a cool event with no follow-up; and we pat ourselves on the back for feeding "those poor people", or doing "good stuff". Many times, we want to simply feel good about ourselves for serving God one day at an event. If we get honest, we might admit that we like occasionally volunteering for events because they don't take much commitment; and then we can control how much we volunteer to ensure it doesn't interrupt our lives too badly.

In the end, we don't make one disciple, but what did Jesus say we are supposed to do? He said to make disciples. If we're going to obey that command, we've got to follow-up with people who respond at an event which makes it what we call, an event with intent.

A common event with intent that we have done within the network is called Hip Hop Hope. At this event, we will have a Christian Hip Hop artist perform, provide food, play games, maybe have a snow cone or popcorn machine, and just hang out to start building relationships. It draws kids because the children are drawn to the music, but it is intended to reach families and build a bridge into the community.

The intent is to find a person of peace, so we follow-up with as many receptive people as we can. We always need to be looking for opportunities to share the good news in new areas, but we also begin looking for opportunities to start these discovery studies. Hopefully, it will then lead to a Body of Christ Gathering, a new church, which will be discussed in a later chapter.

The full picture is that we go into an area and we prayer walk. We look for intel, maybe do these events with intent, and look for a person of peace. Remember that a person of peace should meet the three R's: Receptive, Reputation (good or bad), and Relationally connected. This person, or people, will be the bridge for the gospel to go to a whole bunch of other people in that community. After identifying a potential person of peace, we then try to start the discovery studies to determine the level of receptivity and faithfulness in the area. We ask them if they are open to starting a group in their home, apartment, a clubhouse, or some restaurant. Ultimately, we want to see a Body of Christ Gathering planted in that community, revealing the life of Christ, and reproducing the whole process.

One might ask why we make such a big deal about the Person of Peace rather than just going into an area and starting a Discovery Study ourselves. The problem can be that there are cultural barriers present when an "outsider" comes into a new area. We want to stay away from any appearance of that community needing a hero of sorts to come in and fix them.

Rather, if we can find one receptive person within the community, train and empower them, then the message will likely be more widely received from that person. We want to set the example that Kingdom work is not dependent on one person, but that every believer is qualified and should be living as a disciple-making disciple.

Can you see how that works? We know that within every pocket of people that's in a dark place, there are bridges and there are barriers. Sometimes when engaging the people, it takes us a while to figure out the barriers and bridges. That doesn't mean we don't go, we just go and let the Holy Spirit guide us to figure it out. We have to be okay with making mistakes because we're going to make them. It's all a part of the risk, but it's necessary.

Learning From the Saints Before Us

To close out this chapter, I'll share a story. Billy Graham, who is a well-known evangelist, has spoken in front of a great many people; and many have come to Christ because of him speaking to these large crowds. There's a guy, named Dawson Trotman, who was one of my spiritual heroes; and he was a man who raised up and invested in some sailors. These sailors in turn invested in others sailors. This continued to the point that when Pearl Harbor was bombed, Dawson Trotman could say that him and the rest of his navigators had shared the gospel with every sailor on the ships that went down when they were attacked.

He believed in a big enough vision to think small, and wrote a pamphlet called Born to Reproduce. Someone might be inclined to think that I wrote the pamphlet because it is so close to what I teach, but I did not. He is someone that I have learned a lot from. In reality, all of these principles have been learned from somewhere else because they are all principles in Scripture.

Billy Graham began to see that they were having thousands of people respond at his crusades, but when they left, the communities didn't change. He recognized that they were not connected at a deeper level that led to people following God as reproducible disciples. They were not having an event with intent. So, Billy Graham asked Dawson Trotman to help them follow up, and raise up teams that would follow up with those who came to Christ when the crusade left town.

What happens at these large events is that many people get moved out of emotion, and they really don't understand the decision that they are making. It is good that they come forward to make a decision, but they need someone to help them understand what it means to follow Jesus. They need help understanding who Jesus is, what He's done for us, and what He requires of us. Many people have not been confronted with the cost of following Christ, and this is important for them to know in the beginning.

They need to walk through the Scriptures to know what that means because unfortunately, there will be a lot of people who turn back. I've been doing this now for almost 30 years; and I've seen some people that are good soil and still reproducing today, but I've seen a lot of people that turned back. I'm talking about a lot of good leaders, who had some experience at being faithful and fruitful, but they did not finish well.

I want to see faithful and fruitful disciples who finish well; and I believe that's what God wants to see. That is one of the things that Paul could say – I have been faithful. I have been fruitful. I am going to finish well. That is why he is such a great example, and I believe that's what God wants out of all of us.

Chapter 5
How Do We Invest?
(Multiplying Disciples)

To begin this chapter, let's review the passage in Matthew which is referred to as the Great Commission.

"Then Jesus came to them and said, 'All authority in heaven and on earth has been given to me. Therefore, go and make disciples of all nations, baptizing them in the name of the Father and of the Son and of the Holy Spirit, and teaching them to obey everything I have commanded you. And surely, I am with you always, to the very end of the age."

Matthew 28:18-20 (NIV)

We look at this as the Great Co-mission, which means that we, as believers, are supposed to be together in this mission with each other and with God. We want to align our lives with where God is at work, and we should be supporting each other and working together as a team.

Unfortunately, it seems like a lot of the time, we are on different teams competing against each other for church members rather than working together to complete the Great Commission. My vision and hope for anyone who participates in the trainings I lead, or who is reading this book, is that we partner together. We can do far more together than we can as individuals.

"If you want to go fast, go alone; but if you want to go far, go together."

~African Proverb

It is certainly not realistic to think that we can all work directly together. Meaning that we can spend time together in large gatherings praying, preparing and going into the same fields. But if we are obediently following Christ with a united mind and mission, then we are working together in Spirit and in Truth.

The sad truth is that many are working in the same fields, or pockets of people, but they are not working together. This is divisive, unproductive, and unfruitful; and is the result of a competitive spirit rather than unity.

Now, when Jesus talks about making disciples in the Great Commission, He includes baptism as a step of obedience after someone gives their life to Christ. Evangelism is often talked about as separate from discipleship, but it's all one thing. Jesus is saying, "Go and make disciples…" and when you make disciples, you are leading them to a place of recognizing that they want to be identified with Christ as their King. As they turn from the world and turn to Him, we baptize them as a symbol of their identification with Christ. We teach them to obey immediately. It's all one process.

"Busyness"

In Chapter 3, we discussed the different responses people will have to the Gospel and what our response should be accordingly. Let's say we have someone who wants to follow Jesus, and we lead them to confess Him as Lord. Their confession is only the beginning, and we will want to take them deeper. Let's look at how to do that exactly.

We want to help them multiply the life of Christ that has been placed in them. We want them to share it, and to see it multiply like the good soil (fourth soil) we discussed in the first chapter from Jesus's parable in Mark 4. What did the good soil do? It bore fruit and multiplied "thirty, sixty, and a hundredfold". In the Mark 4 passage, Jesus identified four different soils, so let's look at the other three soils.

The first soil is a rocky path, and as the seeds fall along this path, birds come and snatch them up.

The second soil is shallow; and therefore, is not very effective soil. When the seeds fall in this soil, they sprout up, but burn up quickly by the sun because the roots don't go deep.

I usually describe America as a "third soil" culture, as the third soil very accurately describes our western culture. What happens here is that after seeds fall, they begin to grow and bear fruit; but then weeds and thorns grow up among them without being removed, and the good fruit gets choked out by the cares of this world.

To really get to a place of multiplying disciples here in America, we have to get to a place of changing the busyness in our lives. One of the things I love to say is, "If the devil doesn't make you bad, he makes you busy." Busyness is a real struggle in our culture, and especially within our Christian culture. We keep ourselves busy going from event to event to event; and almost never leave time to build relationships with unreached people, engage them with the gospel, and teach them to obey.

Some real lifestyle changes will be needed to be intentional about obedience, and this is true of urban cultures all over the world. Good soil should be worked, constantly cultivated, for fruit to be produced.

I work with several nonprofit ministries. One of them asked me to come in and help them to reach and multiply disciples, and to equip and send them out. I went to observe for a while; and as

I began to listen (usually it's young people), they were all involved in about six different events. They weren't bad things by any means. However, they were saying they wanted to reach people, yet their entire time was spent going from one Christian event to another, going to concerts, and going to this or that Bible study. In the end, they had no time left to spend reaching out to anyone.

I shared with them the need for an entire lifestyle change. Again, with part of the busyness of our culture being within the numerous events in our church life, we end up so consumed with going to church to the point that we aren't being the church.

Living this stuff out is going to require making some tough decisions. How will we reach people if all our time is spent attending a Bible study or some other program with nothing but believers gathered around praying "Oh Lord, bless us four and no more!" or "We are the frozen chosen. Lord, won't you light a fire in us!"?

Okay, so maybe that's a little sarcastic, and most would certainly not pray that. However, in time, it is easy to end up looking like an inward, "members only" country club instead of a movement of radical disciples.

If we keep doing what we've been doing, we're going to keep getting what we've been getting. If we're not making disciples or reaching the unreached, maybe it's time to make some changes in the habits of our lives. Maybe it's time to investigate the busyness, learn how to take the time to seize opportunities to pray and engage unreached people, and to multiply disciples. That's what it will take to cultivate good soil!

Tre9 (Founder of Eyes On Me, Inc. & leader in M4 Network) and I wrestle with this a lot. We have a lot of guys that are willing to get out of the four walls, and go to outreach events;

but they really only want to help with the event itself. We must maintain the vision that our events have intent.

Remember we discussed in the last chapter that the purpose and intent behind our events is to build bridges that ultimately lead to discipleship. The problem was that volunteers would come to the event; but then when we would have people come to Christ, volunteers weren't willing to go through the discovery studies, follow up or really sit down with them. When you look at a scenario like this, it really begs the question, "Why?!"

Most of the time, the reason is because they don't have time; and sometimes it's even the reason of "I don't have time because I'm going to church tonight." You can see the difficulty this presents, and how this creates a little tension.

I am a huge proponent of gathering in a body. I mean, I am a church planter. However, if all our time is spent gathering, and we're not doing any going, then that's a problem. Part of going means we go and plant the gospel; and when the gospel takes root, we've got to stay there and let the body of Christ be birthed there.

We keep extracting people out of their culture, and then wondering why we are not seeing transformation in their cultures/communities. We keep inviting them back to our buildings rather than meeting with them right there in their homes.

Their networks (People they know, Places they go, Passions they show - Home, Work, Play) are where we should not only be training them and pouring our lives into them, but teaching them to gather and disciple their friends and family. You will see the transformation start happening. That's the model you see in the Scriptures, but we have a tendency to not do it that way in our culture. Now, we should ask ourselves, "Are we willing to die to our comforts and our calendars?"

Practice Activity:

In the last chapter, we discussed how a disciple is much more than just a follower of Christ. Let's take a look in scripture at what Jesus says about a disciple. This is not an exhaustive look at the scriptures, but it will give us a good idea. Read the passages and in twenty words or less, describe what Jesus says a disciple looks like. When considering descriptions, don't allow yourself to get into an argument over words, but keep it simple. We want to avoid "religious language" such as saying, "A disciple is a justified, sanctified, anointed, believer of God."

- John 15:7-17
- John 13:34-35
- Matthew 9:36-38
- Luke 10:1-7
- John 8:31
- Luke 14:25-35
- Luke 9:23-25

Did those scriptures say anything within any of the verses in the list about singing in the choir? Did it say to go to church? As we said before, gathering with other believers is very important; but hopefully you can see that we are simply trying to shed light on how some can be a committed church member, but not be a disciple. The goal is that the two will work together. We want to hold to the idea that our church membership is based upon discipleship.

Below are some descriptions of a disciple you might have pulled from the passages you just reviewed. While we look at these examples, always remember the depth of God's love and grace for us. That is what will motivate us to be the disciples He wants us to be, but we must be willing to lay our lives down. We need to focus on being countercultural rather than doing everything that the culture does. We need to have a willingness to get out there and learn and grow. A large part of learning to live as a disciple, truly is on-the-job training.

A disciple . . .

- abides in Christ, is obedient, bears fruit, glorifies God, has joy and loves community - God's family. **(John 15:7-17)**

- loves others as Christ loves. **(John 13:34-35)**

- is committed to world evangelism and the Father's heart. **(Matthew 28:18-20)**

- is looking for the Person of Peace, praying and going. **(Luke 10:1-12)**

- is committed to Christ's teachings. **(John 8:31)**

- puts Christ before self, family, and possessions. **(Luke 14:25-35)**

- is willing to deny self, take up a cross daily, and follow Jesus. **(Luke 9:23-25)**

"The Church has majored in sin management and the production of religious goods and services geared for Christian consumers."

- Paraphrase of Dallas Willard[viii]

"Christianity without discipleship is always a Christianity without Christ."

- The Cost of Discipleship by Dietrich Bonhoeffer[ix]

On-the-job Training

Below are two very simple ways to think about how disciples are made.

- Model Christ-likeness for them:
    - I do, you watch
    - I do, you assist
    - You do, then I assist
    - You do, then I watch (release)
- M.A.W.L. the disciple!
    - Model
    - Assist
    - Watch
    - Launch

Jesus said, "Follow me." Now, there were some times where he taught in the synagogue, and they saw him teach; but it wasn't in a classroom. He was doing life, getting out there, and living the stuff He talked about. Americans say, "I need to be equipped more" before they're willing to go and do anything; but I always ask them, "Man, how long do I need to equip you?"

In the story about the guy who had all the demons,[23] how much seminary did he have? How long was he equipped? He wanted to go with Jesus; and Jesus told him no, but to go tell his story to the people back in his city. The woman at the well,[24] how

---

[23] Mark 5:1-20
[24] John 4:5-42

long was she equipped? They weren't equipped at all. They encountered Jesus and that was enough.

They obeyed instantly. Immediately. Obedience to Christ ought to start immediately!

Instead, it seems like we would rather sit in a classroom waiting for some light bulb to go off. True learning only happens when we put what we learn into practice. We must get on the job training. It is the only way to truly develop both confidence and competence. That's why it's such a beautiful thing to have someone who is mature walking alongside us to help us out. When our approach to discipleship is, classroom learning only, we never experience true discipleship in the field, and the light is not taken into the darkness!

Another common misconception that keeps us in the classroom is that we feel like we have to clean ourselves up. "If I just get clean enough, I'll do it." I come from a family who loves to fish, and we always say that you don't clean fish before you catch them. When we get "caught" by Christ, He's the one that cleans us up. If you and I try to clean up our act before we get out there, that's ridiculous. We'll never get out there, and we'll never get clean. We need to trust Jesus to clean us up.

Discipleship also involves seeking to understand other cultures or our ministry context.

I mentioned before that, in Ethiopia, there are certain places where I don't wear my cross and some places it's okay. Some places it's a bridge and some places it's a barrier. I never wear my earring; and if you're tattooed, you better be covered among certain people groups because culturally they'll think you're of Satan.

We may be believers and in Christ's grace and freedom; but it's their culture, and we respect it when we're in their land.[25] Those are important things to know when talking about reaching unreached people, and if you're walking with someone a little more mature or experienced, they can help you with those things.

Even so, it is better for you to get out there and discover those things, than to sit in a classroom and just say, "That's good to know! One day I'm going to do it." I would rather you live on the edge of falling and learn from your mistakes. That's better than seeing you stuck in a rut because of the fear of failing or making a mistake. We sometimes call this failing forward; although, it's not actually failing, just the process of learning and growing.

Sharing Life

It is important to remember that the process of discipleship is both teaching others to teach others, and teaching information that may be applied to our lives. We've been saying it's not just a classroom experience. We need to be encouraging this on-the-job training, and living this lifestyle in front of someone. People need to see us in our everyday lives.

Something my wife and I have done for years is have young men live with us that we disciple and train. Many of them have come from broken homes, but in our home, they see what it's like for a family to sit around a table for a meal and engage in conversation. We just talk about our days, and each person has an opportunity to talk.

Did you know that in most homes today, they don't eat dinner together? Many separate and do their own thing. Families are so busy, and it's amazing how few people will engage in a

---

[25] 1 Corinthians 9:19-23

meal and conversation around the dinner table. This is why it's important for people to see us live this stuff out. Paul talks about acting as a spiritual mother and father among the Thessalonians.[26] He said that they cherished and cared for them like a mother, and then they worked hard and lived it out among them like a father. They lived it out with them as spiritual parents.

Empower and Release

While we need to invest deeply in those who will allow us, we do always need to be looking to release people. We tend to create dependency on our teaching, wanting people to need our teaching because we need that ego booster. "I'm the one who's bringing the meat. I am in-depth. I teach line by line, precept by precept. I am the greatest teacher, and you need to listen to me." Please note: I am aware this isn't everyone's motivation.

We need great teachers, but great teaching is empowering and teaching people to teach others. Remember we said that milk is a secondary source; and if you go to an ancient culture like Africa, they will think that if you're on milk, that means that you're still nursing on your mother's breasts. The idea is to no longer need your mom to feed you, and learn how to feed yourself.

When we talk about making disciples, the idea is not for them to get everything from us; but to be learning how to feed themselves in Scripture and to listen to the Holy Spirit. One of the things that we do not allow in our organic churches and discovery groups is for anyone to be the Bible answer man or woman.

What tends to happen in groups where there is someone who has been to seminary or has been a pastor, is that everybody will

---

[26] 1 Thessalonians 2:7-12

turn to that person for the answers when a question is asked. Instead, we need to be sure, as leaders, to be asking people what they think the word of God says. Don't be quick to give an answer, but respond with something like, "What is God teaching us?" Or "What do you think this says?"

Some people have even ended up mad at me for not answering all their questions. I'll tell them to go research that and get back to me, and then we'll talk about it. It's not that I have a problem sharing, or don't want to answer their questions. I want to share with them; but I want them to learn how to feed themselves, and how to leave room for the Holy Spirit to teach them.

We create an unhealthy dependence on us by being the Bible answer man, but we need to point them to Christ and teach them how to feed themselves. We want disciples who are carrying and reproducing the Kingdom DNA everywhere they go!

DNA

Just as our physical DNA carries the genetic instructions that determine our growth, development, and functioning; we have spiritual DNA that should determine our growth, development, and functioning as disciples and God's Church/Family. It is essential that this DNA is incorporated into every method of discipleship or gathering.

It has been my experience that starting with the Kingdom DNA, as a foundation in our church gatherings, is much easier than trying to transition a church to develop the DNA. However, it is possible to begin to infuse the DNA into your church. Life Change Groups are a very simple way to begin this process, and they will be discussed in detail shortly.

Our Spiritual DNA consists of three main elements:

Divine Truth (Read the Word) – The word of God is a witness to the perfect Son of God (Jesus Christ), who should be our focus! We must learn to read and feed ourselves from God's Word.

Nurturing Relationships (Community and Accountability) – Learning in community and confessing our sins and shortcomings. They will know we are Christians by our love for one another.[27] See, the reason why we are a part of the new race; the reason why it was so mind blowing at Pentecost, when the Holy Spirit came, is that all those people came from different backgrounds. They used to hate each other and cut one another down; then suddenly, they started loving on one another in such a way that it freaked everyone out. They started realizing they were a new race under a new citizenship. They were new people. The change in the way they lived and how they treated one another was truly powerful, and it blew people's minds. We are part of that new race; but we've lost it, and we've got to have nurturing relationships to get us back.

Apostolic Mission (Multiplying Disciples Who Make Disciples) – Praying intentionally for family and friends who are far from God and new pockets of people we want to reach. This is going and transforming cultures – being his hands, eyes, feet, and voice with everyone that we meet.

Life Change Groups

A very simple disciple-making system (creating self-feeders) that has been put to the test for years, in many different cultures, is what's called a Life Change Group (LCG).[28] An LCG is based on two or three people (sent ones), contains the DNA, and has high expectations; but is still simple and reproducible, which is

---

[27] John 13:35

[28] LCG is an adaptation from the same author of LTG referenced in Chapter 2

important to see movement. Let's break down what the LCG's look like.

What is a Life Change Group (LCG)?

An LCG is a small group of people who need Jesus to change their lives from the inside out. Peers help each other to follow Christ, and learn how to teach others.

An LCG will:

- Meet each week for about an hour

- Have two or three people in each group

- Make sure men meet with men and women with women

- Need no extra books or training

- Use the Bible to learn about Jesus

- Make sure that all members of the group are equal

Who should be in an LCG?

Two things are important for starting or joining an LCG.

- You acknowledge you have a need for Jesus Christ (Luke 5:29-32)

- You will be faithful to the LCG and how it works (2 Timothy 2:2)

Reading

Members should decide which book or number of chapters in the Bible to read each week. Throughout everyone's reading, they should be answering the Discovery Study Questions mentioned below to help with understanding and processing the reading. If any one member is not able to finish all the reading, all members will read the same assignment again the next week.

It is recommended to work through entire books, rather than selecting small sections and jumping around, so that large chunks of Scripture are read in proper context.

Discovery Study Questions

The Discovery Study Questions have been mentioned before; and are simple, reproducible questions that anyone can use to discuss and discover the Truth of God's Word. It's very easy to use with the six basic questions.

1. What lessons did I learn?

2. What examples will I follow?

3. What promises can I enjoy?

4. What prayers do I need to pray?

5. What is the Character of God revealed?

6. Who will I share my learning with?

You don't necessarily have to use these exact questions, and you may notice that they differ slightly from the questions listed in Chapter Three; but they are a good guide if you are not comfortable making up your own. Work on allowing the Holy Spirit to guide and prompt you with questions that may be more specific to the individual with whom you are meeting.

Life Change Questions:

These are accountability questions, where you willingly submit to one another in fear and reverence for Christ, confess your darkness, and bring it into the light. These questions help us transform and grow as we submit to brothers and sisters in Christ.

1. Have you been a good example this week to the greatness of Jesus Christ with both your words and actions?

2. Have you been truthful about your money and possessions, or wanted something someone else had this week?

3. Have you been nice and helpful to others this week?

4. Have you talked badly about someone else this week?

5. Have you used anything or done anything that you know you should not be doing this week?

6. Have you stayed angry at someone else this week?

7. Have you wished something bad would happen to someone else this week?

8. Have you looked at sex material or thought about having sex with someone you shouldn't this week?

9. Did you finish the reading and learn more about God this week?

10. Are you telling the truth?

Pray Scripture Over Them

The LCG's ask us to identify at least six people who don't know God or are far from God, and to pray Scripture over their lives. For each of the blanks, you will fill in their names. "Lord, I pray that you make __Jim__ want to know you according to John 6:44 and Acts 17:27." Refer back to Chapter Two where we practiced making this list and praying the scriptures over them. We use this same principle to pray over the Ministry Map we made in Chapter Three.

The Multiplication Principle of LCG's

Here is a simple introduction to the principle of multiplication within LCG's. These groups should never have more than three members. If another person wants to join the LCG, then you need to decide who will leave to start a new LCG, making two separate ones. Members should always be ready and willing to start a new LCG.

2 + 1 = 3

But…

3 + 1 = 2 + 2

That's the multiplication process. It's about simplicity and equipping others. It's about keeping things confidential or secret in the group. The groups are made to multiply, and it's easy to get a hold of resources.[29] LCG's are easy and powerful when the principles are properly practiced.

Practice Activity

Take some time to practice going through an LCG, and use Hebrews 5:11-14 for the Discovery Study portion.

DNA in the LCG

Can you see how the LCG is built on the three parts of the DNA?

We seek <u>Divine Truth</u> by reading and learning Scripture together in its context. Now-a-days, we have too much proof texting. I'm a gifted enough communicator where I can basically take Scripture from all kinds of places, and proof text it to write a sermon on how I could beat you up in Jesus's name. I mean,

---

[29] LCG brochures can be ordered at www.cmaresources.org

Scripture says that whatever you do with your hand, you do with all your might,[30] right?!

You can take bits and pieces of Scripture to make nearly any point you want, and that's how a lot of sermons are done. They take bits and pieces of Scripture, and plug them into a sermon, and people believe what they've been told by this "professional". Not everyone has selfish or evil intent behind doing this, but the point is that many Christians will just accept what's taught by teachers/pastors rather than learn how to feed themselves.

If you get people who are reading the Bible together, in its context, we learn more effectively to take the Scripture in its whole. We realize that the Bible is a whole story, from Genesis to Revelation, of God's heart for the nations; and there's a thread running through it that God loves us, and sent us a Savior. This Savior will be the tree of life, in whom we will nourish our lives upon, and through whom He will reveal His life among the nations. It's one story, carried through many books, but all pointing to a relationship with God through Jesus Christ. That's amazing!

Then, in the <u>Nurturing Relationships</u>, we have accountable relationships with one another. What I say to you stays with you. We're going to love one another, but we're going to be honest with one another. One of the problems with our Christian culture is that we are not honest. Many of us are still living in bondage to our sin rather than living in the freedom Jesus offered through grace.

When in bondage, we feel like we cannot honestly tell someone what is going on with us, and act like everything is good. We don't talk about the dark areas that we struggle with because

---

[30] Ecclesiastes 9:10

we are afraid we're going to be judged and condemned. We don't feel like it's safe.

There is certainly a reality that there is a lack of safe places, but someone has to step up and be the one to say, "It really doesn't matter what you do with my stuff. I confess my sins, and as I confess them, that brings healing." Ephesians 5:8-14 says to bring your dark things into the light. James 5:16 says to confess our sins to one another and pray for one another so that we can be healed.

We need to start bringing our darkness into the light, and when we do, it brings healing to our lives. When we have trusted friends, who we can confess our sins to, we can experience healing.

Finally, we are living out the Apostolic Mission as we pray Scripture over our family and friends who don't know God or are far from Him. We recommend keeping your list of family and friends in your Bible or wherever you most often pray to help you stay consistent in praying for them.

Remember, don't just know it – do it!

My challenge to you is to start an LCG with someone in the next 30 days. Hopefully you've seen that the directions are simple enough that anyone can read this and follow it. Now, if someone doesn't know Christ, then you start with a discovery study to help begin introducing them to Jesus. Once they say they want to follow Him, then you begin to enter into the LCG.

We use LCG's in our Network in three different ways:

- Transition: To help infuse the Kingdom DNA into an existing body of believers. A Sunday School, Bible Study, or Small Group could begin the implementation; or it could be a congregation-wide challenge.

- Church Planting: We have seen LCG's initiate the birth of new churches. They are the Kingdom DNA seeds that give birth to a Body of Christ Gathering (church)

- Leadership Development: We have used the LCG's to help develop leaders and leadership communities.

Exhale, Inhale, and Communicate

Neil Cole has said in his greenhouse trainings and writings that we need to exhale, inhale, and communicate. When we go through 2 Timothy 2:1-4, we see that it talks about the disciple-reproduction process; and how Paul invested in Timothy, then Timothy invested in faithful ones who invested in others.

Teach them to teach others! This can't be said enough.

We see this multiplication process that Paul followed. I mentioned how we need to learn how to exhale. That is, we need to learn how to exhale the junk in our lives, the things that are keeping us from Christ.

"Nevertheless, God's solid foundation stands firm, sealed with this inscription: 'The Lord knows those who are His,' and, 'Everyone who confesses the name of the Lord must turn away from wickedness.' In a large house there are articles not only of gold and silver, but also of wood and clay; some are for special purposes and some for common use. Those who cleanse themselves from the latter will be instruments for special purposes, made holy, useful to the Master and prepared to do any good work. Flee the evil desires of youth, and pursue righteousness, faith, love, and peace, along with those who call on the Lord out of a pure heart."

2 Timothy 2:19-22 (NIV)

Turning from our wickedness and embracing the purity of Christ involves our confession of our shortcomings and our struggles. I've been meeting in LCG's for about 15 years, and we have multiplied many of them. I know the type of change that it's brought to my life, and the freedom that I have found in Christ when I'm willing to exhale the junk, but then inhale the good stuff. Inhaling would look like taking the Scripture, internalizing it, and yielding to the Holy Spirit.

"All Scripture is God-breathed and is useful for teaching, rebuking, correcting and training in righteousness, so that the servant of God may be thoroughly equipped for every good work."

2 Timothy 3:16-17 (NIV)

We exhale our junk; inhale truth through the Word; and communicate the gospel by living, praying, and sharing its good news.

"In the presence of God and of Christ Jesus, who will judge the living and the dead, and in view of His appearing and His kingdom, I give you this charge: Preach the word; be prepared in season and out of season; correct, rebuke, and encourage – with great patience and careful instruction. For the time will come when people will not put up with sound doctrine. Instead, to suit their own desires, they will gather around them a great number of teachers to say what their itching ears want to hear. They will turn their ears away from the truth and turn aside to myths. But you, keep your head in all situations, endure hardship, do the work of an evangelist, discharge all the duties of your ministry."

2 Timothy 4:1-5 (NIV)

Notice how the message about what's coming is the absolute opposite of 2 Timothy 2:2? The opposite says that in the end times there will be people who gather around themselves teachers who only gather listeners. They will gather teachers who will simply tell them what their ears want to hear, rather than teaching them to teach others to teach others.

The Effects of True Discipleship

Discipleship should create humility and unity in our lives.

A disciple's life ought to be changed, changed to become more and more like Jesus Christ. We do things so backwards in our culture. In Philippians 2, Paul says that unity is only maintained by Christ-like humility, and that those in Christ have the same mind of Christ. He goes on to remind us about the amazing life of Christ. Although He was God, He humbled himself to enter our world as every human enters the world. Paul says that when we are like him, and consider him and others first, then we'll have unity.

Unfortunately, we don't see this in our culture. Instead, we create bylaws and doctrine, and we think doctrine is going to bring unity. Take an honest step back, and think about how much unity we truly have in this culture. There's a whole lot of doctrine, but there's very little unity. It's only through Christ-like humility that unity can come.

I'm not saying we shouldn't believe in certain things or that doctrine isn't important; but that we should be more focused on believing in Christ and being like Christ. When we are like Him, we humbly deal with people with a greater grace that brings unity to the body of Christ. When we are doctrine-focused, it only divides. If you are a hyper-Calvinist, I can love you and say, "Yeah, God chooses people." If you are Arminian, and say we have choices, I can say, "Yeah, we have choices."

I can genuinely and humbly interact and relate with you both. I don't have any problem with either of those stances as long as we learn how to live with Christ-like humility, and focus on Him

94

as disciples. Paul says this type of mindset will bring unity to our gatherings. We let secondary things be secondary, and keep the primary focus on being like Christ. That is the key.

Thank You, God, for Philippians 2 and ultimately, Christ's example.

Stories from the Field

There are many people who believe in me so much, especially with me being the youngest in our ministry. For example, Guy Caskey, who is in my phone as "Guy Caskey (Triple OG)", invited me to go to Africa with him. When he first asked me about it, I was shocked at the opportunity and how God is pouring into my life. I've only been out of state twice – once to Missouri and once to New Orleans, LA where my sister, Karen, and I went out to share the gospel. For Guy, who is like a spiritual father to me, to invite me to Africa really made me feel so thankful. It is a beautiful thing that means so much to me. On this trip, I plan to learn more about other cultures, about how God is moving globally, and to bring back and teach what I learned to others. Also, I believe I will learn so much from Guy on the way.

- JC Sandoval, M4 Network

I've seen guys that I met in prison, join me on mission upon their release and immediately start learning our way of training and began leading people to Christ. Within 6 months, Ronnie Legg had already baptized his son and others from the hood because he was given the platform and the freedom to share his story. I watched PyRexx go from only being a rapper to leading discovery studies and Body of Christ Gatherings. I took a 17 year meth addict, who completed his recovery at the Manna House in Brookshire, and placed him in our mission house. He began leading people to Christ and has probably baptized more people in his first 18 months than I did in 18 years. I could go on and on about people who have radically changed their lives, some of which were sitting in a church pew for many years, that are teaching people to follow Christ and challenging them to make disciples.

- Bobby (Tre9) Herring, M4 Network

Chapter 6
Why Do We Exist?
(Moving to Healthy Church)

By now, the principles of teaching others to teach others and the multiplication of disciples is certainly not lacking! We mentioned that when you look at the Scriptures, from Genesis to Revelation, one of the things that we see is that God has a heart for all nations. When Jesus went to equip and train His disciples, through the power of the Holy Spirit, He told them to go and make disciples of all nations. He also said to baptize them in the name of the Father, the Son, and the Holy Spirit, and to teach them to obey everything He commanded.[31]

We've talked a lot about the church, and why is it important today. Now, we want to talk about how, when we multiply disciples, the disciples should gather to meet as the body of Christ, which we call a Body of Christ Gathering (church).

We are His Church

I believe the most beautiful creation in all of God's kingdom is His body, which He refers to as His bride, through whom He fills and expresses His life. What we see in Acts 2-3, is the birth of a body of Christ that begins to express His life and all the things that we have been talking about. The multiplication of

---

[31] Matthew 28:18-20

97

disciples is leading up to us functioning together as a body. The question that now surfaces is "How do I lead a Body of Christ Gathering?"

One of the beautiful things we see in the Scriptures is that the Body of Christ Gathering is supposed to be led by the Holy Spirit and Christ Himself. That does not mean that God doesn't use leadership, rather, it's a different kind of leadership. Jesus broke down the religious norms of the day as He discussed leadership with His disciples.

Up to that point, the rulers of the Gentiles led by lording things over everybody; but Jesus explained that it would be different for them, as they would become servants who reflect His very life.[32]

A Body of Christ Gathering begins with disciple-making disciples coming together around Christ as the head and King of that body. Jesus's words to His disciples in John 15 is foundational. He says, "I am the vine and you are the branches." When disciples are connected to Jesus as the vine, He can then express His life in and through them. So, when the body of Christ gathers, the life of Christ should be expressed in and through it.

In this chapter, we are going to provide some tools at how to begin those gatherings. I believe it is God's desire to express His life through Body of Christ Gatherings in cities all over the globe!

I would describe a healthy body of Christ as Christ followers who are sharing their story, sharing the gospel, and baptizing others on a regular basis. As a result, people are being taught the simplicity of the gospel and how to share it with others. A healthy church will give financially towards their vision, take communion regularly, care for one another deeply, keep each other

---

[32] Matthew 20:25-28; Mark 10:42-45

accountable to obedience, raise up leaders that will train others in discipleship reproduction, and launch them into new churches rather than stay in the same place.

- Bobby (Tre9) Herring, M4 Network

Let's look at a passage together that talks about how God's eternal purpose has been to express Himself through the Body of Christ Gathering.

"Although I am less than the least of all the Lord's people, this grace was given me: to preach to the Gentiles the boundless riches of Christ, and to make plain to everyone the administration of this mystery, which for ages past was kept hidden in God, who created all things. His intent was that now, through the church, the manifold wisdom of God should be made known to the rulers and authorities in the heavenly realms, according to his eternal purpose that he accomplished in Christ Jesus our Lord. In him and through faith in him we may approach God with freedom and confidence."

Ephesians 3:8-12 (NIV)

The Three-Thirds Process
(A Guide for Our Time)

Like everything else we have been doing, an important principle about a Body of Christ Gathering is that it should be kept simple so that it can be more easily reproduced. We tend to make church or discipleship very complex. Really, it should be simple enough that any believer could lead a gathering in any environment.

In the Body of Christ Gathering, there are three parts, and time for each part will depend on the length of your gathering (i.e. If you meet for 30 minutes, each part would be 10 minutes). We call this the three-thirds process, and this tool helps establish

99

the DNA in every method of gathering (discipleship, training, church, etc.).

Look Back – *Nurturing Relationships*

1. **Care (How are you?)**

   a. Care for each other (Sometimes it's helpful to break into groups of 2 or 3 to care and pray for one another).

      i. Ask for the Highs and Low's of the week

      ii. Share how God has been at work

      iii. Ask how you can pray for each other and spend time praying

   b. List out needs within your church and community to pray over and evaluate as a church how you can be involved in meeting the need.

2. **Worship**

   a. Read a Psalm or sing a song. A musician is not required for singing songs. Sing from your heart and don't worry about how it sounds. Though there is a musical element and it's nice to have instruments, it's not required. Worship is simply adoration and praise to God, and is not meant to be a showcase of someone's talents. There may also be the option to play a song from a device if there are available means.

   b. Taking the Lord's Supper together is another great way to worship.

   c. Brag on God. Share the great things you have seen God do throughout your week.

d. Have everyone go around and fill in the blank, "I would like to thank God for _____."

3. Did You...? (Accountability)

At the end of the Three-Thirds you will see that we set goals for accountability, and they are called "I will's".

    a. Did you complete your "I will's"?

    b. What do you need to confess and surrender?

    c. What is something you have learned from Scripture this week?

4. Remember (Vision Casting)

    a. A paraphrase of Proverbs 29:18 is that without a vision, people will perish. In this part, we want to keep our vision in front of us so that we don't grow stale and complacent.

    b. The vision is the Father's Heart:

        i. All Scripture, from Genesis to Revelation, reveals that the Father's Heart is for <u>All Nations</u> (Gen 12:3; Rev 5:9)

        ii. God will accomplish this through <u>Transformation</u>. He gives us a new heart and a new identity. (Ezek 11:19; 2 Cor 5:17)

        iii. The fruit of transformation is <u>Multiplication</u>. As our lives are transformed, we teach others to teach others. (Matt 28:18-20; 2 Tim 2:2)

        iv. Multiplication leads to <u>Generations</u> of disciples and churches being planted (John 17:17-21; Acts 2:37-39)

    v. All this until there is No Place Left where the Gospel has not been proclaimed and reproducing churches established in every nation. #NoPlaceLeft (Rom 15:23; Acts 19:10; Matt 24:14)

Look Up – Divine Truth

New Lesson in the format of a Discovery Study.

Look Forward – Apostolic Mission

1. Practice

Use this time to practice learning and teaching a simple tool, or to put into practice something learned during the New Lesson (i.e. If the lesson was about praying, have everyone practice praying out loud).

2. "I will…" (Set Goals)

We set two types of goals here:

a. One goal is what we call a "grow" goal that will challenge us in our personal growth and spiritual maturity. This may include committing to read your Bible daily, pray daily, memorize scripture, practice a certain discipline to correct a character issue, etc.

b. Another goal we set is called a "Go" goal, to help keep us accountable to always move forward, pursuing the Father's Heart. This may include asking yourself where there is a place you would like to see a body of Christ gathering started, who you need to contact from your ministry map, going in pairs to a new area to prayer walk and share, how many times you would like to share your story

and/or His story as you go throughout your week,
etc.

3. Pray

Pray over and commission one another as you head out into
the harvest fields throughout the week.

Remember that, at the point we're starting a Body of Christ
Gathering, we've shared our stories, we've shared His story, and
we have disciples who want to gather in order to reproduce this
whole process all over again. The purpose of this simple,
reproducing process is to see communities transformed, and
Christ revealed in cities and nations around the world.

Once we've got four to six people who are now disciples of
Christ, we're going to do our first gathering around Christ and
His Word. This can be done with two or three people as you
move toward healthy church. Just remember that critical mass
(the number of people gathering) is important for sustainability
and longevity.

Practice Activity:

As you see, the Three-Thirds Process above is broken up
into three parts so that it is easy to follow. Our hope is that you
can experience an example together on how to lead a Body of
Christ Gathering, so take some time to practice and see if you are
able to follow the instructions. Allow the Holy Spirit to use
creativity and gifting as you worship, care, etc. See the bullets
below for specific instructions on certain pieces.

- For "Accountability" in the first third, ask the following
  questions

  a) Who shared their story or His story this week?

  b) Did you pray over your ministry map?

c) Did you train anyone in any tools you've learned so far?

- For the "New Lesson" in the second-third, read Ephesians 3:7 – 13; Acts 16:6 – 15, 40 and Philippians 4:14 – 19; and then ask the questions below.

  o What did you like about the story?

  o What did you learn about God?

  o What did you learn about the person of peace and pockets of people (Oikos)?

  o What did you learn about making disciples and church planting?

  o What do you need to obey or change after studying these passages?

- For "Practice" in the final third

  o Each person practice writing out the elements of the Three-Thirds process from memory.

  o Take some time to debrief as well. You've just spent time practicing and being an example of a body of Christ gathering. What did you like? Who can lead one? What do you think would be difficult about leading one?

- For "Prayer" to close the time, spend time praying over one another, and the people and places you would love to see a body of Christ gathering birthed.

Any time that we are helping someone or teaching someone to teach someone else, we need to give them an opportunity to practice doing it. That's why we encourage you through each of these steps to take time to practice. If you are practicing in a group, be sure to allow time for discussion afterward about what was learned and experienced.

Keep in mind, we aren't claiming to have all the answers (or the best); but we do have access to missionaries all over the globe, who are sharing the "best practices" and tools that they have learned by experience (with lots of failing forward). Tools are very important to the process; therefore, we are sharing many of them with you in this book with hopes that you too will embrace the Father's Heart and the No Place Left vision. However, be sure to do some research, find out what is working in your context, and always be a humble learner.

Feedback from the Field – Body of Christ Gathering

Trainee 1:

It's easy. I led one this past Sunday, and I was definitely nervous at first. Afterwards, I wondered what they thought about how I did and what they thought about me; but I just had to trust that I was obedient to what God wanted me to do. I trust that He's going to do all the work, and I just have to speak for Him.

Trainee 2:

It really showed me how simple it is because these questions that we are answering about the Scripture passages are the same questions we use every week. We don't have to get fancy with the kinds of questions we're asking. We can let the Holy Spirit do the teaching on how this is church. Whenever I thought of church planting before, I thought about the only formula of church that I knew – where we have a gathering, a music service, a message by one pastor, everyone sits and listens, and then we adjourn. That formula has been shattered for me. That's not church. Church is just people coming to learn from God. The three thirds process simplifies it and makes me feel a lot less anxiety from thinking, "Oh, I have to do all of this stuff to plant a church; and worry about 'What if we don't have the musicians?' or 'What if we don't have a sound system?'" So this just shows me how simple being the church really can be.

Trainee 3:

I like how we take smaller bites of Scripture. You're not taking in so much at once, and you're getting a more complete teaching of what the Holy Spirit is trying to teach. He speaks to us all a little bit differently. Instead of there just being whatever I'm getting from it, there's also whatever he's getting from it and whatever she's getting from it. We're getting a more complete view of what God has intended.

Less Programs, More Discipleship

One of the major influences in my life is a guy named Neil Cole. One of the things that he says is that we need to simplify, or lower the bar, in the way that we do church, and raise the bar of our expectation of discipleship.[x] The Body of Christ Gathering, using the three-thirds process, allows for that. It is a simple process that has high disciple-making expectations built into it.

An interesting point about church planting is that, in the New Testament, you see apostles and prophets on these teams that were sent out. It even says the foundation of these churches was catalyzed by apostles and prophets.[33] I believe part of the reason those specific gifts are used is that the prophets provide a lot of the Spirit-led intel that points everyone to the need to listen to, and go where God says we need to go. The apostolic gift provides more of the strategic pieces. All of us need to listen to

---

[33] Ephesians 2:20

God, but I think that's a great example. We just need to make sure we are listening to God's Spirit and His direction, and follow where He is going.

Putting the Pieces Together

The passages of Scripture in the example of the Body of Christ Gathering were intentionally chosen to line something up. Notice that we started out talking about how the mystery that God revealed to Paul was the reality that God wants the body of Christ to reveal Him in every city on the face of the globe. He says that the body of Christ is to reveal who He is even to the heavens.

Then we were able to see this worked out as we looked at Paul and his team heading into Philippi. They were going to look for receptive people; and they found Lydia, who is very receptive. Because of Lydia's receptivity, her whole household/network is receptive. It's worth noting that a prophetic vision was given earlier to the team to head to Macedonia, instead of Asia, which lead them to Philippi in the first place.

Right after Paul and Silas left Lydia's house, they were confronted by a female slave who had a spirit of telling the future, and she was used by her masters to earn them money. She followed them for days and Paul got so annoyed that he cast the demon out.

The slave girl's masters were not happy since she was a source of income, so they took Paul and Silas to the officials, who then severely beat them and threw them in jail. As they were singing hymns and praising God in this prison, God broke their chains along with everyone else in the prison and opened the gates. The Philippian jailer was about to kill himself because he thought everyone escaped, but Paul and Silas stopped him and let him know that they were all still there. Through this they shared the gospel with him, he cleaned their wounds, and then he and his entire Oikos (Household) believed in Jesus.

I believe the Philippian jailer may have been the man who showed up to Paul in the vision to say, "Come to Macedonia."

This is a powerful story to show once again that in every city and every pocket of people, there are people of peace that God wants to use as bridges of the Gospel; and ultimately, to see the multiplication of disciples and the body of Christ gather together.

As Paul and Silas were leaving town where they had been imprisoned, they stopped at Lydia's house where there was a gathering going on. The believers prayed for them, and sent them out on their way. We find out later in the book of Philippians that it was the church in Philippi who funded the rest of Paul's mission from beyond Macedonia and stretching into Asia.

In Asia, there are leaders developed at Tyrannus, who are connected to the church in Ephesus. Acts 19:10 tells us that all of Asia heard the Gospel because these disciples engaged in a disciple-making process. Paul even makes some changes in his strategy in Ephesus, or further develops it, to focus on training indigenous leaders to go out to the rest of Asia. Out of that, we see that the entire book of Revelation is addressed to the seven churches in Asia.

He uses leaders from each of the regions he journeyed through to cross pollinate with each other. In Acts 20:1-6, we see that there were leaders from Galatia, Macedonia, and Asia with Paul when he was in Greece writing the book of Romans. He states in Romans 15:23 that there is now no place left in the regions for him to work. Why? Because he developed leaders who were committed to the Kingdom and the reproduction of disciples, and church planting movements had begun in multiple places throughout the region.

We see this powerful process that started with a person of peace named Lydia, who decided to follow Jesus. A Body of Christ Gathering began in her home, and then they sent out apostolic leaders to take the gospel out of Macedonia and into Asia. What a beautiful picture this paints on how the body of Christ is to work, to equip, to send, and to reproduce.

Reproducing Churches, Not Just Disciples

The whole idea of all these principles and tools is that the Body of Christ Gathering is to reproduce everything that has been presented. When we gather, we need to be urging one another to engage people by sharing our stories and sharing His story. Discipleship needs to happen, not just one-on-one, but also in groups, including within the Body of Christ Gathering.

That means that churches who reproduce other churches are how God's eternal purpose will be fulfilled – till the Glory of Lord fills the earth according to the Prophetic word given to Habakkuk.[34]

Some communication on discipleship implies that it only happens one-on-one. While one-on-one discipleship is good and beneficial, it's important when you're meeting with someone, to bring them into a church gathering where they can see the body of Christ functioning together.

This allows them to see that you are not just special (or crazy), but that there is an entire body affirming the very things that you've been teaching them. The discipleship process is holistic, meaning that there's one-on-one discipleship, but then the body of Christ brings affirmation as they gather and function together.

---

[34] Habakkuk 2:14

The large group gatherings, the discipleship (one-on-one or with multiple people), the story sharing, the going out, and the sending is all working together. We will never get to the end in mind with just one-on-one discipleship. We must see multiple streams of churches reproducing generations of churches to accomplish the Father's heart of having people from all nations before His throne.

Therefore, getting to a Body of Christ Gathering is not the end. We've been talking about the idea of living out reproducible discipleship. We don't end with the start of a Body of Christ Gathering. It's intended to be reproduced repeatedly until cultures and communities are transformed.

In the final chapter, we will look at the whole picture being revealed throughout the previous chapters, and how it is a reproductive cycle.

Jesus said to go therefore to all nations. Remember how, in Acts 1:8, Jesus's instructions were to start in Jerusalem, and then a movement happened as those Body of Christ Gatherings reproduced and sent people out. The gospel ends up being taken from one location to the next, and one culture to the next – from faithfulness in little to faithfulness in much.

Reviewing Movement from the Harvest to a

Body of Christ Gathering

When starting out with someone in an unreached area, where there are new people coming to Christ, we recommend using simple stories. We have a story set that helps people focus on the commands of Christ that will help them grow as disciples, as well as lead them to begin gathering and moving toward becoming a healthy church.[35]

We start off by using the short-term discipleship story set[36], and make sure that the meetings continue to be participatory. Participation is one of the things that we ignore in our culture because we're so used to didactic teaching, which simply means there's just one person teaching. When you read 1 Corinthians 14:26, Paul says that the churches that he plants are built on the foundation of Jesus Christ, participating together, and prophesying over one another. (See also 1 Cor. 14:3) We see through this that everyone has a responsibility to participate.

What I tell our guys is that they should treat the gathering as if there is a plate of cookies in the center of it, and everybody gets one. Sometimes there are difficulties with someone who dominates by talking and talking and talking. If you're the one starting a church, it's not your job to talk the whole time. Your job is to facilitate participation. Some of us love to hear ourselves talk; but it ends up being too much, and we don't facilitate the process. So, make sure that groups are very participatory.

Remember the three layers in these gatherings.

The "D" which stands for Divine Truth is discovered as we spend time LOOKING UP in the Word and focusing on Christ.

We have a time of Nurturing Relationships, the "N", where we check on how everyone is doing by LOOKING BACK. We care for one another a little bit; and spend time in worship through music, reading a Psalm, or simply thanking God for the things He is doing. We hold each other accountable; and we have

---

[35] Appendix E – Short Term Discipleship (Based on Nathan Shank's Four fields manual and Steve Smith's T4T)

[36] Story sets can be adjusted based on your context or preference; however, we would recommend a minimum of four story sets.

a time of vision casting, where we remind each other of why we exist, that we can only do this by His power, and that we need to keep moving forward.

Finally, we talk about the "A" of going and obeying and commissioning one another, which is the Apostolic portion where we LOOK FORWARD. How are we going to apply what we learned in the gathering? Where do we need to go to take the gospel, multiply disciples, and see the body of Christ formed? What goals are we going to set to help us obey?

This is the Kingdom DNA that must be reproduced in every field of development, in every tribe, tongue, and nation.

The reason we ask people in the first layer to share the ways in which they obeyed God (which may be based upon the previous meeting or based upon what they've been reading in the Word) is because Jesus didn't say to simply go and teach lots of information. He said go and teach them to obey.[37] We willingly submit to one another in accountability because it helps fuel the obedience God requires or weeds out those who are not serious about growing as a disciple.

That means we need to be okay with submitting to one another. Accountability shouldn't be an obligation. If there is a feeling of obligation or being "lorded over" then we've misunderstood. We ought to welcome accountability, and it should include a celebration of what God does through obedience as much as tough love when we aren't obedient. Sometimes we'll be able to say that we're doing pretty good, but we need to be humble and teachable enough to acknowledge when we are disobeying.

---

[37] Matthew 28:19

Remember that we talked in the last chapter about confessing those things through the LCG process. We need to have a solid understanding of our identity in Christ that allows us to readily admit when we're not doing very well. When we can do that, it allows other believers to encourage us to do well.

The Core Four

If we look more closely at those three layers, they are made up of eight parts.

First Layer (Look Back)

1. How are you?

2. Worship

3. **Accountability ("Did you")**

4. **Vision Casting (Reminder)**

Second Layer (Look Up)

5. Teaching

Third Layer (Look Forward)

6. **Practice**

7. **Set Goals ("I will")**

8. Pray

Within those eight parts, there are four parts that we call "The Core Four" which are in bold type above. These four things provide strength and sustainability for the multiplication of disciples and church planting movements. This reveals something very interesting.

If you look at most church gatherings, we typically only do four of the eight parts. Usually the four that we do in most church settings are teaching, worship, prayer, and caring for one another. Now, those are certainly good things, but the issue is that there is not as much effectiveness in multiplying disciples when we only do these four. The DNA is not complete so it does not reproduce.

Multiplying disciples is about obedience in intentional relationships. It's about casting the vision to help others catch it; and it's about being accountable to put into practice the stuff we read, talk, and pray about.

When we say that it's important to practice, we're not just talking about just practicing in a training group time. We're talking about going out into the fields where we model these principles and have people watch what we do (e.g. How we eat around the dinner table with our family, how we love our wives, how we do our singleness in purity, how we share our faith, how we train, how we disciple, etc.). Whatever "life" we do, we invite people to come along with us to watch, practice, and eventually do what we are doing.

We can invite them into our Body of Christ Gathering where they can participate and practice. If they don't know how to pray, we should teach them how to pray by practicing; and can lead them by saying, "To pray, just fill in the blank here: 'God, I thank you for ____.' and 'God, I ask you for ____.'" Start them out with simple, reproducible ways that they can practice.

Setting goals simply means understanding where we are, where God wants us to be, and what the little steps are that we need to take to get there. We have a vision, which is the preferred future of where we want to go, and we have the current reality of where we are. We need to then determine what steps are necessary to establish a sort of vision path to move toward that preferred future.[38]

The Core Four are essential principles that help reproduction and multiplication that moves forward more quickly.

Healthy Church Circle

What does a healthy church look like anyway? Is healthy church something we simply try to achieve as though we are seeking to "arrive"? Hopefully, the answer to that is clear by now, that the work of a disciple and the church is never done while we are on this earth. We will constantly be in a place of moving toward healthy church because the cycle should always be reproduced. One of the tools we use within the network and the No Place Left coalition is called the Church Circle.

As a group of disciples begins to gather (even if it starts with two), we want to identify it as a church. The stick figure identifies the number attending. The cross identifies the number of believers. The water identifies the number of people baptized, and the parenthesis is for the number of believers who have baptized someone.

In Acts 2:36-47, we see the first church formed. From that list, nine elements are seen that make up a healthy church. (The

---

[38] Appendix F – Growth or Transformation Vision Path

Three T's by the dollar sign for giving stand for Time, Talent, and Treasure. Jesus didn't just ask for our money. He asked for all of us.

As a church, we then determine which of the elements we are doing and move them into the circle. This helps us then identify what areas we need to work on. There may only be a few inside the circle in the beginning and that's okay. Remember, moving to healthy church is a process!

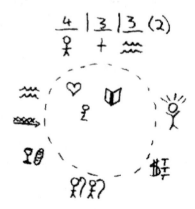

At some point, it is important that the church identifies itself as a church. Those gathering need to covenant together as church. That just means they are committing to working together as a church to move toward healthy church, to submit in mutual, loving accountability… to become family.

When this happens, we draw a solid line around circle instead of a dotted line, even if all the elements are not yet present.

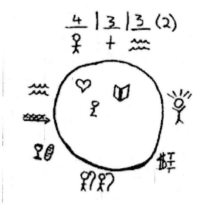

Wrapping Up

To wrap up this chapter, we hope to tie some things together. We've talked about the importance of the person of peace and of the Oikos (or relational networks). When we look at a city, such as the city of Houston, we need to view it as a network of relationships. Imagine a web of interconnected relationships, where people are less than six steps of separation from each other. We will then discover connecting hubs, tribes, unique passions, and people groups that help form the complex web of a modern urban city.[39]

---

[39] The complexities of a modern city are covered in Chapter 2, page 34.

We need to view the place we want to reach as a network of relationships. In our culture, we tend to think of our city in the mindset of institutions and corporations, rather than thinking about it as a network of relationships.

I'll give you a beautiful example of my father, who was the head of intelligence for the state of Texas when 9/11 happened. He worked for the Department of Public Safety; and was over all the special crimes, kind of like the CIA but at the state level. Because of that event, he said that, in intelligence all over the United States, they learned that they relied too much on technology and institutional intelligence rather than peoples' intelligence. They lost their ability to relationally penetrate a cell or a group of people in order to build relationships to gain information (i.e. intelligence).

This is our call as missionaries! When we consider the apostolic call, we see Paul describing himself as a sort of "holy chameleon". He explains how he became a Jew to the Jews, a Greek to the Greeks, and all things to all people so that by all means he might win some.[40]

So, he's saying that he would go into a place and learn that culture in order to build the gospel bridge to it. Remember how we talked about Paul's time in Athens, where he noticed their religious culture as he walked around? He acknowledged their statue to the unknown God, and started quoting their poetry. That's amazing!

Likewise, we need to view the areas we want to see reached as a network of relationships, where we learn their culture to bridge the Gospel. Remember that in every pocket of people, in our home cities and in any unreached culture, there is a person of peace, or even multiple persons of peace that will be a bridge

---

[40] 1 Corinthians 9:19-23

for the Gospel! There are affinity groups or tribes in every city that God wants to use to help connect people so they can experience community.

When we find this person of peace, and they come to Christ; then the gospel flows to all these others within their oikos and discipleship starts happening. As those people start gathering together as a body of Christ, their oikos becomes an oikos of God or an oikos of faith.

In Galatians 6:10, that is exactly what that verse says, that particularly among the household of faith, or the oikos of God, God's desire is to see that person of peace be reached. Through them, the gospel will flow to other people, who will be discipled through a process and form Body of Christ Gatherings all over the world. So, let us not become weary in doing good (sowing seed) because in due season we will reap a harvest that will lead to a household of faith (oikos that is the church) if we don't give up![41]

The discipleship process is a process for developing leaders. In every field, from engaging people all the way to church formation, we want to see people growing, learning, and developing as disciple-making disciples of Christ.

Jesus himself said the harvest is plentiful, but the laborers are few, and to ask the Lord of the harvest to send more laborers into the harvest field. Then Jesus turned and told his disciples that he is sending them out as lambs among wolves.[42]

That doesn't sound like a very promising place to be as a lamb; but when you're following the good shepherd, you are assured of being under his care and leadership. The good shepherd will lead us into the fields where we will find lost sheep

---

[41] Galatians 6:9-10
[42] Luke 10:2-3

being harassed by the wolves, and they will become future kingdom leaders.

As we work our way through the fields and develop, we will become disciples of Christ, who not only have gifts but become a gift per Ephesians 4:11-16. These leaders are what the next chapter is all about. We need an intentional leadership process that develops people in these ministry gifts.

Chapter 7
What's The Problem?
(Maturing Leaders)

Before we dig into this final chapter, let's review everything we've done up to this point. In Chapter Three, we talked about napkin theology, which just means using tools that are simple enough to be written on a napkin and reproduced from here to the sands of Somalia. These tools can be used in both one-on-one and group trainings.

Look at the Four Fields chart and think about it being like a clockwise lifecycle. Like the water cycle in biology, there is a disciple-making cycle; and you can write it all on one page using the Four Fields tool. The four fields of Kingdom growth will help us connect with God's organic process.

"And the LORD answered me: 'Write the vision; and make it plain on tablets, so he may run who reads it.'"

Habakkuk 2:2 (ESV)

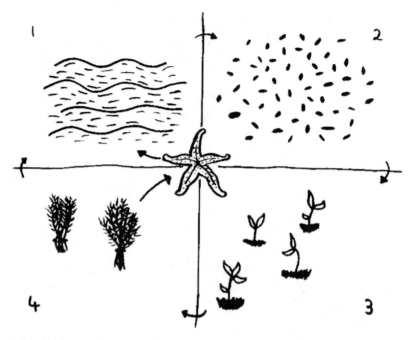

The first box of the Four Fields chart[43] begins with sharing "My Story"; and we talked about where we should go, and how we enter new fields (entrance strategy). From there we move from sharing "My Story" to the second box with sharing "His Story" (what to say and do). Here we start talking about who to invest in, and how to begin the discipleship process and establishing the DNA.

In the third box, we look at how to dig in deeper with discipleship and multiplying disciples. Finally, once we start multiplying disciples, they start gathering together to form a Body of Christ Gathering. This gathering of believers is the word "church" in the Bible. Church is a group of people who are following Christ, and identify themselves as a church by covenant (baptism and The Lord's Supper). Once the Body of Christ

---

[43] The Four fields manual was compiled and written by Nathan and Kari Shank

Gathering happens, this church is supposed to reproduce the cycle.

The mind-blowing reality about this "process" is that it is all happening at the same time, and is not nearly as clean and sequential as we may like. However, for the sake of learning and intentionality, it is taught throughout the No Place Left coalition that there needs to be a posture of abiding, a process of Kingdom reproduction and a path using simple tools.

Developing Leaders

In the center of the Four Fields chart, there is a starfish. There is a story behind the starfish, which will be shared later in this chapter, but we use that to symbolize the community of leaders and trainers. This community of leaders and trainers is what we will focus on in this chapter. If we want to see multiple churches start faithfully meeting, we need to have maturing leaders who meet together to encourage one another, to build one another up, and to keep one another accountable to seeing this process multiplying.

We can use five phases here to describe the four fields process:

1. Ministry – These are the people, places and passions God wants to see transformed

2. Message – This is communicating the Gospel in a clear and reproducible way that is modeled

3. Multiplying Disciples – This involves the growing and training process, as well as moving people to being a healthy church

4. Moving to Healthy Church – This involves learning to function and identify as a healthy church

5. Maturing Leaders – This involves investing in maturing leaders who become a gift back to the body by building them up and equipping them to continue the reproducing cycle

Each of these phases has a tool that goes with them:

1. Ministry – Ministry Map

2. Message – Three Circles and Discovery Groups

3. Multiplying Disciples – DNA (Three-Thirds Process), Identity, Short Term story set, Timothy Map

4. Moving to Healthy Church – Generational Mapping, Church Circle, Three-thirds Process

5. Maturing Leaders – Leadership Church Community, Iron-on-Iron, LCG, Timothy Reading Plan, Three-thirds Process

As we mentioned, this final chapter will talk more about "maturing leaders" with equipping gifts from Scripture and how they function. The people who make up this group of leaders are men and women who have these equipping gifts and have matured spiritually. We will discuss how they help the process go even faster.

Practice Activity:

Look at the blank Four Fields chart below, and see how much you can fill in from memory. Just fill in everything that you can remember for each of the boxes. Think of tools, principles, illustrations, examples, etc.

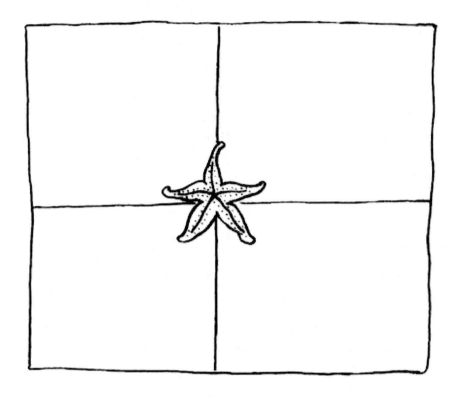

Review of the Four Fields

In the first box, we talk about sharing our stories and asked "Where do we go or who do we share with?" This is all about how we engage people and enter new fields of ministry. If we are going by ourselves, we can go to our Oikos/Relational Network, which is our family and friends (use ministry map tool); but if we are going into a new pocket of people or an unfamiliar territory, then we need to go by two's.

In the second box, we move from sharing our story to sharing His story (i.e. the Gospel). We communicate the message

125

through the Three Circles, which serves as a filter to find where God is at work. Through Discovery Studies we share simple story sets like the Four Stories of Hope and allow the Holy Spirit to reveal Himself through His Word.[44] Another option is to go through one of the Gospels of Matthew, Mark, Luke, or John. Personally, my favorite to start with is John.

One of the things I like to do when going through Scripture with someone is to have them journal using SOS – What does it Say? What do I need to Obey? What do I need to Share? That is just a simple way for them to process and apply the Scriptures as they are reading, and helps when we come back together to talk about it.

When we are determining who to invest in, we use the acrostic F.A.I.T.H. We take this from Paul identifying Timothy as his son in the faith.[45] When someone really wants to be a disciple-making disciple, they'll be:

Faithful – When given something to do, they do it (i.e. asked to read a designated amount of Scripture and they read or asked to share their story with someone and they share).

Available – They make time in their schedule to have regular meetings and keep those meetings. It doesn't stop just at being available for meetings; but also available emotionally, ready to share life and be in the harvest.

Initiative – They are consistently reading, showing up, obeying, repenting, etc. If there is a time you forget to give them some assignment or goal, they take the initiative to ask you rather than wait to be told.

---

[44] Mentioned in Chapter 4 – Appendix C
[45] 1 Timothy 1:2

Teachable – They sincerely want to learn and wanting to grow. They receive and welcome loving correction and accountability.

Hungry – Those who hunger and thirst for righteousness are filled. They must want it enough to do it. Many people want something, but aren't willing to do what it takes to achieve it.

In this process, we allow God to choose Timothy's based upon their obedient response to the commands of Christ. I use to try and identify those who I would invest in by my own perceptions. Of course, my tendency was to choose the most gifted, affluent or talented. After making a lot of painful mistakes, I started letting God choose them based upon their faithfulness to Him. Thus, I have seen a lot more fourth soil disciples who will reproduce other disciples.

In the third box, we talked about the DNA of God's Kingdom, and about multiplying disciples. Remember, the DNA of God's kingdom stands for:

Divine Truth – The Word of God points to Jesus, who is the holy Son of God, the divine truth

Nurturing Relationships – Caring for one another physically, emotionally, and spiritually

Apostolic Mission – Getting out and living the Great Commission, and forming bodies of Christ that are expressing His life.

Finally, in the fourth box, we addressed how once we start multiplying some disciples, then we gather them together, which is called church. We saw that God's eternal purpose, based on Ephesians 3, is to see disciple-making disciples formed together as a body of Christ (church), in every city all over the globe. That is His strategy for building His Kingdom. Remember that a

127

simple beginning for a Body of Christ Gathering has three layers (three-thirds), each representing a leg of a three-legged stool or throne our King Jesus sits upon.

Look Back! (N) – Worship, Caring for one another, Accountability, and Vision casting

Look Up! (D) – Time in the Word, pointing to Christ

Look Forward! (A) – Practice, Set Goals and Pray

Out of those eight parts, we talked about the Four Core values (Accountability, Vision, Practice, Setting Goals) that generate stronger effectiveness in reproducing disciples, and how they are left out of most of our churches or small groups.

Accountability may be disregarded so as not to offend anyone or to avoid the mess of walking with people through growth.

We don't give people a **Vision** or allow them to be empowered by releasing authority to them. We seem to overlook having a vision of God's ideal, and how He wants us to join Him.

We need to not only **Practice** in a group of other believers; but we should start practicing outside of the safety of our Christian environments – in the streets, in a house, or a restaurant, etc. Most other things we do require practice and training, but it's typically left out of our spiritual growth.

Finally, we tend to neglect **Setting Goals**. One of the interesting things that comes up in my conversations with friends, as we work with a lot of pockets of poverty, is that many people in poverty don't set goals or make daily lists. However, this discipline is essential for determining one's destiny. I believe this a great tool to fight poverty with, and is so important in the learning stages of reproduction to keep us growing. We not only need to be able to identify what we need to do, but we need to be able to set realistic goals that will help us accomplish it.

What do we typically do in all of our small groups or churches? We study God's word. Is that bad or wrong? No, that's a good thing! We pray, worship, and care for one another, which are all very good and important and scriptural.

So, what's the problem if we are doing these good things? The problem is that those are all only inward focused. When we leave out the other pieces, we leave out engaging with those who don't know Christ. Few people are bold enough to walk into a service or Bible study on their own. According to George Barna, a majority of the population won't even come by invitation of a trusted friend. If we're not engaging and reaching new people, we end up only recycling believers instead of multiplying and reproducing new disciples.

Stuckology

One of the other benefits of this whole process is that it helps us with something I like to call, "stuckology" (I first heard this from Jeff Sundell, former missionary to Southeast Asia and pioneer of the T4T movement here in the West). It means that when a group is in that stage of meeting together in a Body of Christ Gathering (church), they sometimes get stuck. All churches will get stuck in their lifetime and all of us get stuck from time to time in our individual disciple-making process.

Many churches will reach a point where they've been together for a year; but haven't really reached anyone new, or made any new disciples. It is helpful to use the Four Fields chart as a tool, to go through it from the very beginning to help determine where the process broke down. I will ask questions in line with all the principles and tools we've been discussing.

- What does your church look like as it gathers and goes?

- Is everyone sharing their story (engaging people)?

- Is everyone sharing His story (Sharing the Gospel)?

- Are you meeting in a three-thirds process or LCG's (Kingdom multiplication DNA)?"

Sometimes, they'll say yes to those so I'll dig a little deeper...

- How often is everyone praying over their lists of people who don't know God or are far from Him? (Ministry Map)

- How often are you asking each other if you're sharing your story or His story?

- Is everyone sharing in the facilitation and participation?

At that point, the response turns out many times to be "no". They'll say that they have just been talking about their struggles, which is good, but they end up leaving out all the other important parts.

Remember the DNA of God's kingdom. We tend to be all about Divine Truths and Nurturing Relationships, but what we need is a good kick in the "A"! (As Neil Cole has said) We can't leave out the Apostolic Mission. We need to be personally sharing our faith, challenging one another to share, and sending people out into the harvest fields.

Developing leaders means remaining faithful to the Kingdom DNA. Leaders are best developed in the context of the four fields, which includes the local church gathering. When someone takes on the responsibility of being a caring leader (Elder) within Christ's church, they immediately immerse themselves in an environment of transformation.

Q & A – Characteristics of a Healthy Church

What does this environment look like? What is a healthy church?

We define a healthy church with five C's:

Christ – He is the head and foundation of the church.

Covenant – People need to agree to be His church, and commit to Christ and one another.

Characteristics – A healthy church prays; baptizes; makes disciples; teaches the word; participates in the Lord's Supper; Worships; Gives of time, talents and treasure; displays the "one another's" or body life – some would call this fellowship; has caring leaders.

Caring Leaders – Just as families have leadership, churches need caring leaders (Elders) because they are family

Children – Just as families have children, healthy churches should be reproducing other churches

How do you develop and equip leaders?

As mentioned in the beginning of the chapter, when multiple churches start faithfully meeting, the need to gather leaders for leadership development comes into the picture. The reality is you can't even get to multiple churches without leadership development. That's why the MAWL (Model, Assist, Watch, Launch) process is important; but as multiple generations of churches are birthed, there is a big need for mature believers to come together in community as leaders. Forming a leadership community provides an environment for higher accountability and further teaching and equipping. This also serves as a filter for those who are not being obedient or are unable to take on the responsibility for a time.

131

What is a mature believer?

The maturity of a believer has nothing to do with a title or being appointed to some position. Now, sometimes when someone is put into a position, they'll become mature to meet the requirements of the position. That's a good thing, but it would prove to not be very effective as a regular process.

Jesus told His disciples that the greatest in His kingdom will be a servant; and He said, through the apostle Paul, that there are mature servants who grow to such a place where they become a gift back to God's body to help it grow and mature.[46] These mature servants have already developed as five-fold ministers of movements, and we used a starfish to describe their function.

The Starfish and the Snake

Let's talk about the starfish in the center of our reproducing cycle. The Scriptures say that Jesus Christ is the head of God's body in the church, and that Jesus Christ is the foundation. In certain places, we will elect, hire or appoint one person who we consider to be the head, rather than pointing to Christ. That looks a little more like a snake, and the way to kill a snake is to cut the head off.

We see repeatedly in our culture how we look to some dynamic leader. How many churches have disbanded or fell apart after the removal or fall of its leader? In seminary, I was taught that a church should take on the ethos (personality), or charisma, of its leader. That sets everything up to rise and fall primarily upon leadership. Leadership is important, but I believe Christ-like, biblical leadership looks different.

When we look at 1 Corinthians, Paul addresses that there was a problem of divisiveness. There were some wanting to follow

---

[46] Ephesians 4:11-16

him (Paul), some wanting to follow Peter, and some wanting to follow Apollos. He did not try to convince everyone to follow Him, but told them that Jesus is the head of the church.

He planted churches to teach them how to trust in Christ. When we teach people to focus on Christ, and they start maturing; then Christ gives these maturing leaders back to the body to further mature it. This becomes more of a picture of a starfish rather than a snake.

You may have heard the story before of a young boy who kept getting starfish in his nets as he was fishing. He got frustrated, and started chopping them up and throwing back in the water; but they just regenerated and reproduced. You can't chop off a starfish's head!

Persecution Fuels Movement

When you see, movements happen in places like Africa and Asia, when they try to kill the leaders to stop the movement, what typically happens? It typically grows and reproduces even more!

I'm a native Texan, and have been in Houston since I was five years old. I don't know if you have ever experienced the bite of a fire ant, but they're mean. Fire ants can respond in seconds to something dead on the side of the road. Now, we've tried to kill the fire ants, and have spent millions to do it. It has been found that when a mound is in a benign environment (meaning there are no pesticides trying to kill them), the queen ant just chills and reproduces at a normal rate. However, when you start throwing out pesticides, multiple beds start to come together; and the queens work together to reproduce at a rate 300 times their normal rate. So, in a benign, apathetic environment, they do not rapidly multiply; but when you put them under tension and persecution, they very rapidly multiply.[xi]

The church is a living organism too, and we can see it spread and multiply like wildfire (or fire ants) in persecuted environments. There is no room for apathy, game-playing, or just sitting around like a happy little ant bed out there when everything is cool. No, when persecution comes, they start reproducing more rapidly. The point of the starfish is that if you put Christ in control, allow him to be the head, and point people to Christ; we will produce and reproduce leaders who will help it grow and multiply.

The reason why I push to keep things simple, and to get back to the basic Body of Christ Gathering (move to healthy church), is so that we can make and multiply more disciples. We want to see the fulfillment of Jesus's vision for No Place Left and for His Glory to fill the earth![47]

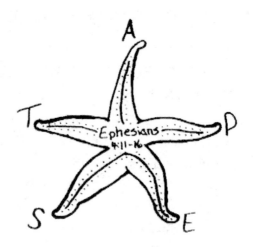

---

[47] Matthew 24:14, 28:19-20 and Acts 1:8

Instinctive Nature

Let's look at one last example from God's creation. This example Illustrates to us why I believe that the environment matters to all living things. God created an environment, called His body, for people to grow. When you take a whale, and put it in a tank, or take a lion and place it in a cage, they begin to lose their instinctive nature. They forget that they are predators, and forget how to feed themselves. They forget how to communicate with other lions and whales. These two animals instinctively operate within their pride and pod, but now they no longer know how to function in a pride or a pod when they have been removed from their habitat (environment).

Can you see what I'm trying to say with these examples? American culture is very individualistic, and we don't know how to function together in community or connect with those who are still far from God. When we are in a healthy body of Christ, I believe we will reproduce more and more disciples because that is the habitat that God intended us to live in. We will live out the instinctive things that He's put within us, such as community and being disciples. We will see the fivefold gifts, revealed in Ephesians 4, working!

Most people haven't even been taught the fivefold gifts (Starfish), nor do they know if they are gifted in one of them. We seem to skip over the entire fourth chapter of Ephesians! We know about a pastor, or shepherd, and we know about a teacher in our culture; but we seldom know about the others. Okay, maybe we'll even throw some evangelists in there, but we don't teach about the role of the apostle and the prophet.

Scripture says that the foundation of the church is laid by apostles and prophets.[48] They have unique roles that we need to

---

[48] Ephesians 2:20

help us start and build churches. So, let's look more at Ephesians 4, and how important it is to see these gifted men and women who will serve as equippers to help us grow and multiply.

"But to each one of us grace has been given as Christ apportioned it."

Ephesians 4:7 (NIV)

Organic Systems vs Business Positions

I want to preface the following section about gifts by acknowledging that there are a lot of opinions, throughout the different denominations that could lead to a lot of varying arguments; but I would like to address what I see in the Scriptures. There are various gifts that are addressed in Scripture. Some are referred to as being gifts of manifestation, which just means the revealing of God's power.

Others are called motivational gifts, meaning there are things that motivate us. If you're a servant, you want to serve. If your gift is administration, you want to administrate. Those are motivational things; but then we have these ministry gifts, and that's what we're looking at. A Body of Christ Gathering (church) needs these ministry gifts to function in different places, and different phases of its growth, to mature.

"Therefore, it says: 'When He ascended on high, He took many captives and gave gifts to His people.' What does 'He ascended' mean except that he also descended to the lower, earthly regions? He who descended is the very one who ascended higher than all the heavens, to fill the whole universe. Christ Himself gave…"

Ephesians 4:8-11 (NIV)

136

Take note that this passage is saying that Jesus is the giver. There are other gifts identified in Scripture, called the gifts of the Holy Spirit; but here we see that Jesus Himself is giving these gifts.

"So Christ Himself gave the apostles, the prophets, the evangelists, the pastors and teachers, to equip His people for works of service, so that the body of Christ may be built up until we all reach unity in the faith and in the knowledge of the Son of God and become mature, attaining to the whole measure of the fullness of Christ. Then we will no longer be infants, tossed back and forth by the waves, and blown here and there by every wind of teaching and by the cunning and craftiness of people in their deceitful scheming. Instead, speaking the truth in love, we will grow to become in every respect the mature body of Him who is the head, that is, Christ. From Him the whole body, joined and held together by every supporting ligament, grows and builds itself up in love, as each part does its work."

Ephesians 4:11-16 (NIV)

Remember we said that Jesus is the one who gives gifts to the body. I believe this is saying that these equippers are men and women who grew to a place of maturity; and that, as they focus on Christ, the Holy Spirit is the One who is helping them to mature. As they grow and mature, Christ gives them to His body to help the body grow and mature.

These people are gifts that Jesus gives. They are mature Christ followers, who have proven themselves through a lot of experience over time to be Faithful, be Available, take Initiative, be Teachable, and be Hungry (people of F.A.I.T.H.). The interesting thing is that we will think of these people as positions that we need to appoint, rather than systems in the body of Christ. Your body has different systems (i.e. circulatory, respiratory, skeletal, etc.) functioning to keep it running. Each of the systems has a unique function.

These maturing leaders are continuing to grow, but they are considered mature because they have gotten out into the fields and walked through the Kingdom multiplication process. This can't happen in a classroom! A classroom can encourage and support, but it provides no hands-on experience. True growth and maturing can only happen as they suffer and persevere as sent ones. They have learned to function by design – God's unique design for them.

So, they have engaged people, and shared the Gospel in the field. They have discipled and gathered people who have had the Gospel take root in their lives (good soil). Then, they have identified proven and practicing leaders who will reproduce the process until there is no place left.[49] These leaders have learned by true experience out in the field.

In our culture, we tend to think of church as being like a business, and we appoint positions. This directs us to pursue people who have all kinds of talent on the exterior, but they can have zero character. That doesn't happen all the time, but it does happen. Jesus says, however, that in His body, it is through mature Christ followers that He helps the body mature. These people are gifts to the body of Christ and function as systems that help it grow in the same way our body has systems that help it grow.

Why is it that we ignore these things? I do not know, but it is part of our culture that we don't address this stuff. I believe it is essential, though, for a multiplying body of Christ, in a place

---

[49] Romans 15:23

138

where Jesus is free to be the head and foundation, that this happens organically or naturally.

We don't have to tell our body that our heart needs to pump. We don't think about needing to appoint a heart to do the pumping. It just happens as we grow. God made us this way!

Fivefold Ministry Gifts

When we are in a culture that is not full of interferences, such as teaching without practice, repetition or application, or things that are not necessary like programs, we see the church blossom and multiply. The equipping gifts function organically or naturally because God created them to do just that. We need to recognize that in, our culture, there are certain interferences or things that will choke this out.

The biggest interference is that we have had pastors and teachers as the sole emphasis. Pastors and Teachers have a very important role in the Kingdom, but they are just two functions, or roles, out of five. We wonder why we are not going and multiplying, but it is because the apostle and prophet are the gifts that lead us to go and multiply. Not all pastors and teachers operate in this way, but it is very common.

We would call this an interference because, when the emphasis is solely on the Pastor and Teacher roles, we end up staying within the four walls of a building. The message becomes, "Come and grow with us" and we end up only trying to gather people in the building rather than wanting them to go. When that happens, we have no need for what we would call the "Go Team" which are the Apostle and the Prophet. The Evangelist is sometimes on this team as well, but we'll discuss that further in a moment. We are not trying to say these gifts are now more important than the ones that have been emphasized, rather that we need to honor and encourage all the gifts and their functions.

When we look at the New Testament, in every team that was sent out, almost every single time, we find that there is someone who has the gift of the apostle and someone who has the gift of the prophet. That's why they are part of the "Go Team". Think about when Jesus said that we need to put new wine into new wineskins.[50] The apostle is constantly pointing us to the wineskin needed to carry the wine to the nations. Meaning we need God's Spirit, His direction, and creative vessels to accomplish the Kingdom work. Often, it was through prophetic words that God gave the direction needed for the apostolic band or team in the New Testament.

Now, we can all be super spiritual and say, "All we need is God, and all I do is follow the Holy Spirit." My response to things like that is that God is both super and natural. If we want to have a vertical relationship with God, we must have a horizontal relationship with people. Imagine if we had a huge container of wine that could bring joy and healing to our city. We decide we want to get that wine to the whole city of Houston, and the world. How are we going to do that?

Well, we would need containers, and those containers are the wineskins. So, the apostles come up with simple, reproducible ways for people to work together in taking the gospel to unreached people, where it can multiply and reproduce. That is how the super and the natural (our relationship with God and our relationship with people) work together.

It takes mature people to work together, and recognize the value in all gifts. What can happen is that the apostle and the prophet may irritate each other because the prophet is always saying how we need to hear from God, and the apostle is saying

---

[50] Matthew 9:17

how we just need to reproduce from here to the sands of Somalia. Can you see how this can become a problem?

I'm a real entrepreneurial person (Apostolic), and I love seeing new things started that are reproducible and sustainable. You will often hear me say, "just stick to the process, utilize the tools and let things work out." I certainly want to hear from God, and the prophet can help me with that; but let's not forget that we need simple, reproducible ways to go out into the fields.

Many nonprofits, or para-church ministries, have been started by Apostles, Prophets and Evangelists because the church was functioning in a way that did not honor their roles. It has only been within the last four or five years that I have been around some really mature, prophetic people, who see how we need to work together. Through our partnership, we are seeing incredible results as we go places together. We must create teams that have a culture of honor where all gifts and functions are honored and valued.

Let's discuss a little more about these fivefold gifts to help us better understand each one of them.

Apostle: An illustration that can be used to identify the fivefold gifts is fingers on a hand. The Apostle is kind of like a thumb, in that it can touch all the gifts. If you drop an apostle in a culture, he would be able to pastor and shepherd people, he would evangelize, God would give him a prophetic word, and he could teach.

Prophet: Can you take a guess at what finger the Prophet would be? They are the pointer finger because they point us to God. Sometimes, like Nathan the prophet to David, it would be pointed in our face; but the prophet helps these Body of Christ Gatherings (church) learn how to hear from God, and how to prophesy over one another.

In 1 Corinthians 14, Paul said that when we gather together, one of the key things we should learn to do is to prophesy over one another. Now, we tend to think of prophesying as being a little weird and hokey in a lot of our circles; but Paul goes on to explain in verse three, that it is simply encouraging, building up, and comforting.

Many people feel the need to walk on eggshells around prophets because they are afraid of being "called out"; but that is not the purpose of the gift, or the way a healthy Body of Christ Gathering should function. We need to build each other up. The only time, in the setting of a Body of Christ Gathering, that we should call someone out, is if a person does not respond to being confronted one on one with a clear sinful pattern. Then we need to follow Matthew 18 and bring it to the entire church. We do not allow people to call each other out during a Body of Christ Gathering for anything other than Biblical church discipline with the intent to restore rather than to punish.

I've dealt with many prophetic people, young ones mostly, but even some old ones who are young in Christ, that regularly call people out in a group setting. I have had to pull them aside, and tell them to keep their mouth shut or not attend if they are going to continue to rip people. (see 1 Corinthians 14:32)

Evangelist. Most of the time, the evangelist would be considered as being on the "Go Team", but I like to call him a "tweener". What I mean by that is that he is in between both teams, so he is like the middle finger. We need a "Go Team" to be the foundation layers, and a "Grow Team" who builds upon that foundation. He needs to help the body of Christ by teaching them to go evangelize, and to share their faith to grow the team.

He is on the "Grow Team" because he helps the body of Christ grow to do what God has called it to do and reproduce;

142

but he's on the "Go Team" too because he helps the body of Christ go out.

The evangelist tends to be extremely extroverted, and the prophet tends to be introverted. I do think, however, that over time, some of us extroverts grow a little more introverted as we get older – or at least that is true for me. I was extremely extroverted when I was younger; but have grown to be more and more introverted over time.

I will jokingly say: "I love people, but I like my dogs a lot better than I like people after spending so much time with them." Sometimes being and working around people can get kind of tough, but we have to keep on loving them even when we may not always like them. That is just some raw truth that I have experienced after years of working with all different types of people.

Getting back to the point, we're just saying the evangelist is usually very extroverted, and they can very effectively draw people in. They are what is referred to as a "people person."

Shepherd: Next up, we have the Shepherd (or Pastor). From my perspective, this is where we have really messed some things up in our culture. In Scripture, the function of the Shepherd/Pastor is to gather people into groups, to love them, to care for them, and to teach them to care for one another. If you were to line people up, describe the functions of each of the fivefold gifts, and then ask them which gift they identify with, most would choose the pastor.

Why? We need people to care for people! It is one of the most important things we do because Scripture says that they, the world, will know that we are Christians by our love for one another and how we function together as a family.

143

The pastor or shepherding gift is the most common equipping gift. It is represented by the ring finger because, in our culture, that finger holds the ring which represents a marriage covenant. The reason why the pastor function is so important, is that it helps the body of Christ learn to covenant together as a family.

"A new command I give you; Love one another. As I have loved you, so you must love one another." John 13:34 (NIV)

There are times where we will see conflict between the pastor and other gifts. I have a friend who is very pastoral. Sometimes I will have conversations with him where I feel like he's keeping me from "going" because he's trying to make sure that everyone is good and okay. I'm like, "Man, I'd rather blow up and go than to have all this pastoral, hugging each other, and holding it all together!"

But we need to work together. I need to listen to that guy because there are times where, if you go too quickly, you could blow the whole thing up. Through this, we can see the need for maturity and Christ-like character to deal with one another.

Teacher: So far, on the "Grow Team", we have the evangelist and the pastor, and the last one is the Teacher. The teacher is that little pinky finger because it can get in every little crack and crevice. A teacher loves to research more than anything. They are constantly focusing on the details of scripture that can help us get deeply rooted.

Story from the Field

I've had the privilege of being used in all of these gifts, however, it is not because I wanted to. It seems that God allowed me to operate in all five gifts in order to spark a movement and gain momentum, but now He has sent me those who are carrying the load. Here is an example of how things have been working. I, apostolically, went into 5th Ward with a vision to see community transformation through multiplication. I decided going to one of the worst parts of the hood in the middle of the night with a series of "Disciple the Streets" hit and runs would be how we would infiltrate. This part of the block was full of dealers, addicts, prostitutes and everything imaginable. I called in a rapper/street disciple named PyRexx, who I knew was prophetic, meaning he proclaimed the word boldly and fearlessly in the streets. He could also relate to that lifestyle. After doing four DTS hit and runs over the span of about six months, God opened a door. Jay Castro, an evangelist who had attended a few of those outreaches with us began reaching out to local businesses and churches in the area. The opportunity to use a local church/business parking lot was presented. Within two months we were there hosting our Hip Hop Hope Tuesday outreach efforts. We saw over 20 people baptized within a six month time span. We connected with a brother named Racy, whom I met in the Carole Vance prison unit, who was open to pastoring a house church. He had already been trained in prison by the other leaders in our network in the principles of multiplication. He and a few others began meeting on a weekly basis, teaching each other and serving at Hip Hop Hope afterwards. This was the clearest picture I've had of Ephesians 4:11-16, in the exact order as they are listed.

- Bobby (Tre9) Herring, M4 Network

I want to remind you that, in every one of these roles, there is a responsibility for them to teach someone to teach others. The apostle has a responsibility to raise up other apostles, and the prophets, the same thing. I believe that all of us, who are believers, latently have each of those gifts within us through the Holy Spirit; but very few of us mature in those gifts to the place where we actually become gifts back to the body. Those who have matured and function in the fivefold gifts are indeed a gift to the body.

I believe that these gifts are what we call trans-local, meaning they work across many different places and cultures, and not just in one place or environment. We will see them function and train in one local body; but once they get to the level of growth and maturity that is described in Ephesians 4, I believe they will be working with multiple Body of Christ Gatherings (church networks) as equippers.

The church needs maturing and developing leaders that help it function in sending (Apostles), hearing (Prophets), sharing (Evangelists), caring (Shepherds) and teaching (Teachers).

Proven Worth

Though I know this can be argued, I want to share my interpretation and my theory on these servants. We see these equippers maturing into the work of a servant that is described in Ephesians. In 1 Timothy 3, it describes elders who function as the mature people in a local body, and then talks about the servants, which is the same word used for deacons. Jesus said that the greatest in His kingdom will be a servant,[51] which is the same word that we see in Ephesians 4:12, where it says to prepare people for works of service.

I believe that 1 Timothy 3:10 is describing what these trans-local ministers look like; and it says to not allow them to be servants, meaning serving the body trans-locally, until they've been tested and proven over time. We don't see that among the requirements for elders, but that's just one of my theories. So, the Elders are affirmed and appointed by the local body, but the deacons have more of a trans-local role, and must be proven and tested.

I wouldn't want to argue about that; but I think we use the term deacon like they are junior assistants or business trustees, when I believe they are supposed to be one of the most mature

---

[51] See Mark 10 and Matthew 20

and experienced people in the kingdom. Although, none of this is really about positions, it is about functions; and that is the point that I want to make.

Ideally, what should happen over time is that as these mature servants start growing, they start helping all the local churches grow. We do need to have meetings sometimes. We can see evidence of leaders, with many of these gifts, gathering together in Acts 13. Here, Paul and Barnabas, an apostle and a prophet, were set apart to be sent out from Antioch. They kept going back to Antioch over and over again, resending out and resending out.

We need times where we learn together, and talk about what's going on. When you have multiple leaders and multiple Body of Christ Gatherings, it is important that those leaders are called together for support, learning and training. We call these Leadership Communities or Communities of Practice. Another good example of a leadership community is in Acts 19 in the Hall of Tyrannus.

One of the first churches I planted reproduced until it was made up of about 15 house churches or cells in the suburbs. Over time, we tried to institutionalize the fivefold gifts in our gatherings, in a local setting. What I mean is that I tried to pick staff based upon these fivefold gifts, and it was a disaster. Instead of me allowing Christ to raise them up, I tried to control it.

My heart had good intentions, but it was a dysfunctional attempt at best. All of this is not something that you can just control or institutionalize by appointing positions. It's something that happens over time. A word of warning: paid positions can make a mess of things. There is a place for pay, but we need to make sure it's given at the right place. As I heard Neil Cole say, "Don't organize it until you have it to organize!"[xii]

It becomes easier to recognize these gifts once you've been around people a long time. The body of Christ, and other mature believers, can affirm their gifting; but any appointment is based upon the affirmation of the body as they see these leaders function maturely in their gift. When someone is functioning in their gift, they are learning to be who God created them to be and this takes time to discover.

This is how I believe Elders were "appointed." It was done in community with the consensus of a local body who agreed about the character of the Elder. Again, we can see these character descriptions in 1 Timothy 3 for more established churches and Titus 1 for churches that are young. Timothy was serving a body that was older and more mature than the body Titus was serving.

The church should affirm its elders and the gifts of its members. We don't need a specific spiritual gifts test to affirm who people are in the body of Christ. What we need is a group of people, who are close knit together, where they know one another; and can affirm those gifts in one another.

In the Bible, there is not a book that has a gifts test. It tells us plainly the gifts are given, and the body of Christ can affirm them. Let me qualify this by saying that I am not opposed to spiritual gifts tests; but even if we take a test, we still need other Christ followers to affirm the gifts. We do not see anyone in Scripture, that was sent out as a go team, who was not sent out by the body of Christ. Therefore, our gifts should be affirmed in the body and by the Holy Spirit too.

Learning from Paul

One of the last things I would like to discuss in regards to leadership are four phases of leadership development. Keep in mind, you may discover someone who is further along in the process. Rather than expecting to start in the first phase, you will want to help them identify where they are and how to get to the next phase. If we look at Paul's life and his missionary journeys, we can observe and glean much from his development.

Phase 1 Direction Modeling	Phase 2 Coaching Assisting
Phase 4 Delegating Launching	Phase 3 Supporting Watching

Phase 1: On his first missionary journey, we see a young man working with Barnabas who had the zeal and desire to get the work done. All of us, when we are young, need the hands-on experience; but there is also often a youthful desire to be the one to do the work ourselves. This is a necessary step for us all, but it limits our ability to multiply and father movements. Therefore, I believe the Galatia region continually had problems, and needed lots of follow up and strengthening compared to the other movements.

During this phase, we need a lot more **directing and modeling** from other mature leaders to help us develop and mature. Getting tools that provide handles to get the work done is very important in this phase of a developing leader's life.

Phase 2: We see Paul, on his second journey, begin to develop the wisdom of building teams. He developed a team that was learning together out in the fields, and was providing leadership for the new churches that were birthed.

During this phase, leaders need **coaching and assisting** as they develop the discipline necessary to build a healthy functioning team. There is a need for lots of encouragement and helpful tools to build the confidence that is necessary to be an equipping leader.

Phase 3: On Paul's third missionary journey to Asia, we see Paul developing or fathering local indigenous leadership. We see Paul shifting in his role, or function, from a super spreader of the Word, who is always out in new fields, to a master trainer who teaches others to engage new fields.[52] It is a joy to see people come to Christ, and it is with great joy that we celebrate birthing a church; but it's the greatest joy to help someone else birth a church until all have heard.

Here is where we see deep maturity by learning to die more to self as a disciple or church. The role as parents, or catalysts of movements, in turn, helps mature the body. This phase in leadership development is where **supporting and watching** is necessary to finish the race you have started. We must have spiritual parents in a movement to empower others to fight the good fight.

Phase 4: While Paul was imprisoned in Rome, in his letter to the Philippian church, he stated that greater progress of the Gospel had occurred.[53] Paul seems to be saying that he has been

---

[52] Acts 19:1-10
[53] Philippians 1:12-14

very effective even while being locked up. Wow, meditate on that for a second! He would even say to Timothy, "so that through me the message might be fully proclaimed and all the Gentiles might hear it."[54] Paul learned to die in such a way that Christ lived through him day by day, so that future generations will obey!

At this point in the maturation process, we see the need for lots of **delegating and launching.** Faithfulness and fruitfulness have been demonstrated over time, and the leader is looking to finish well.

In the No Place Left coalition, we use a great tool, originally developed by Nathan Shank, that describes the different levels of leadership, and that can be found in the appendix.[55]

The Role of Leadership Communities

Leadership development is both an art and a science. It involves both creativity and principles. I believe it is very important to be able to help people determine their current reality (where they are in the growth process), and then give them a vision for a preferred future. Then they need steps or goals, a vision path if you will, that will help them take the necessary steps to move forward to maturity.

Tools help us help others get a handle on things that seem beyond their grasp. These tools help them build the confidence necessary to get out in the fields and move forward in their leadership. Developing as a leader cannot happen without learning to persevere through suffering. A leader should be faithful, fruitful, and in the process of finishing well.

---

[54] 2 Timothy 4:16-18
[55] Appendix G – Levels of Leadership

One of the most important truths about developing leaders is that it happens in Christ-centered community. Again, we see the importance of having a leadership community, or church, that is constantly reflecting on the seven Kingdom activities of Christ.

1) Abiding

2) Vision of the Father's Heart – the "Why?"

3) Engaging People

4) Sharing the Kingdom, the Good News

5) Making Disciples

6) Gathering and Going as the church

7) Leadership Development

Our leadership church has assigned reading, and we ask ourselves where in the reading we see these principles at work. Then we constantly evaluate ourselves on how we are personally doing with these commitments. We do this during the "Looking Back" part of our gathering. As you can see, our leadership church follows the Three-Thirds Process so that the Kingdom DNA is caught in our leadership development process. So, we have gatherings and groups for pre-Christians, then we have a process for new believers and developing leaders.

Leadership is caught more than it is taught, but you need both formal and informal settings for leaders to be developed at their fullest potential. Instead of balance, many programs operate in extremes and err on one side or the other. Some have too much classroom in their process, and others are too unintentional in living life together. We need both.

Closing

Jesus told His leadership team that the harvest is plentiful, but the laborers are few, and that they should ask the Lord of the harvest to send laborers out into the fields. Then, He sent His team out as lambs among wolves.[56] We must follow His example.

He tells us that apart from Him we can do nothing. We must abide (totally trust Him) if we want to bear fruit that lasts. Along the way, there will be a lot of pruning and disciplining to get us to bearing much fruit that lasts. We are to be a Tree of Life (Jesus the Vine and us the fruit bearing branches) in every tribe and tongue, and bring healing to the nations until there is no place left. We are born again to reproduce![57]

---

[56] Luke 10:1-3
[57] John 15; Revelation 22:2

Bibliography

Chapter 1

i C.S. Lewis. *The Chronicles of Narnia: The Lion, the Witch and the Wardrobe.* United Kingdom: Geoffrey Bles, 1950

ii The Matrix. Warner Bros. Pictures, 2001. Film.

Chapter 2

iii Bruce Olson with James Lund. *Bruchko and the Motilone Miracle.* Lake Mary, Florida: Charisma House, 2006

iv Bruce Olson. *Bruchko.* Lake Mary, Florida: Charisma House, 1978

v Neil Cole. "The Life Transformation Group System by Neil Cole." CMA Resources. May 19, 2009. Accessed January 5, 2015. https://www.cmaresources.org/article/ltg

Chapter 3

vi Grown Ups. Sony Pictures Home Entertainment, 2010. Film.

vii 1989, Carol Davis, Tom Wolf and International Urban Institute – Leaf-Line Initiatives

Chapter 5

viii Dallas Willard. *The Divine Conspiracy: Rediscovering Our Hidden Life in God.* HarperOne, 1998

ix Dietrich Bonhoeffer. *The Cost of Discipleship.* New York: Touchstone, 1995

Chapter 6

x Neil Cole. *Organic Church: Growing Faith Where Life Happens.* San Francisco: Jossey-Bass, 2005

Chapter 7

xi Richard Pascale and Mark Milleman. *Surfing the Edge of Chaos: The Laws of Nature and the New Laws of Business*. Reed Business Information, Inc., 2000

xii Neil Cole. *Church 3.0: Upgrades for the Future of the Church*. San Francisco: Jossey-Bass, 2010

Appendix A

My Story

Name_____

My life before I came to Christ:

_____

_____

_____

_____

_____

How/When I came to know Christ:

_____

_____

_____

_____

_____

How my life has been different since I've come to know Christ:

_____

_____

_____

_____

_____

156

Appendix B

Strategic Prayer Focus

Write Names of Family and Friends (those you know) who are far from God:

1.

2.

3.

4.

5.

6.

Strategic Prayer Focus

1. Lord, I pray that you draw _____ to Yourself. (John 6:44)

2. I pray that _____ will seek to know You. (Acts 17:27)

3. I pray that _____ will hear and believe the Word of God for what it really is.

(I Thessalonians. 2:13)

4. I ask You, Lord, to prevent Satan from blinding _____
    to the truth.

(II Cor. 4:4; II Tim. 2:25-26)

5. Holy Spirit, I ask you to convict _____ of his/her sin
    and need for Christ's redemption.

(John 16:7-14)

6. I ask that You send someone who will share the gospel
    with _____.

(Matthew 9:37-38)

7. I also ask that you give me the opportunity, the courage,
    and the right words to share the truth with
    _____. (Colossians 4:3-6; Eph. 6:19-20)

8. Lord, I pray that _____ will turn from his/her sin and
    follows Christ.

(Acts 17:30-31; I Thess. 1:9;10)

9. Lord, I pray that _____ will put all of his/her trust in
    Christ. (John 1:12, 5:24)

10. Lord, I pray that _____ will confess Christ as Lord,
    grow in faith, and bear much fruit for Your glory. (Rom.
    10:9-10; Col. 2:6-7; Luke 8:15)

Appendix C

Stories of Hope

➤ The Sinful Woman (Luke 7:36-50)

➤ The Paralytic (Mark 2:1-12)

➤ The Tax Collector's Prayer (Luke 18:9-17)

➤ The Lost Son (Luke 15:11-32)

Discovery Study Questions

• What did you like?

• What did you learn about God?

• What did you learn about people?

• What would you change after reading the story?

• Who do you want to share with something that you learned today?

Appendix D

Field 1 and 2 Bookmark

"THE HARVEST IS PLENTY, THE WORKERS ARE FEW...PRAY."

LUKE 10: 2

WHO?

LOOK FOR A PERSON OF PEACE:
Oikos
Go --> 2x2

WHAT?

3 QUESTIONS:
Miracle / Prayer?
Far or Near?
Can I tell you a story?

RESPONSE

⬤ LOVINGLY KEEP LOOKING

⬤ 4 STORIES OF HOPE:
Can we meet again?
Sinful Woman (Luke 7: 37-50)
Paralytic (Mark 2: 1-12)
Tax Collector's Prayer (Luke 18: 9-17)
Lost Son (Luke 15: 11-32)

God?

Don't do?   To do?

People? Share?

⬤ GIVE IDENTITY (2 Cor. 5: 17-21)
Train on Oikos Map
Train on Your Story / God's Story
Meet Again and Disciple Them

160

Appendix E

Field 3 Bookmark

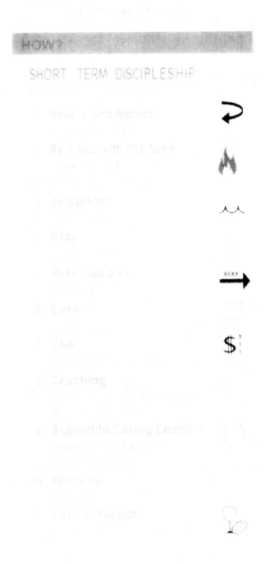

"GO...MAKE DISCIPLES OF ALL
NATIONS...BAPTIZING THEM AND
TEACHING THEM TO OBEY."

HOW?

SHORT TERM DISCIPLESHIP

Believe and Repent

Be Filled with the Spirit

3. Be Baptized

Pray

Make Disciples

Love

Give

Teaching

Submit to Caring Leaders

Worship

Lord's Supper

Appendix F

Growth or Transformation Vision Path

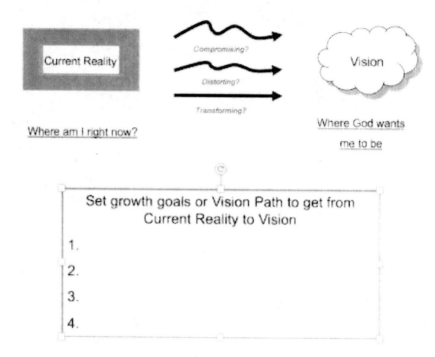

Appendix G

Levels of Leadership

Level 1	Level 2	Level 3	Level 4	Level 5
Seed Sower	Church Planter	CP Multiplier	Multiplication Trainer	Movement Catalyst

Level 1	Level 2	Level 3	Level 4	Level 5
Abide in Christ!	Abide in Christ!	Abide in Christ!	Abide in Christ!	Abide in Christ!
Passion/vision (Why?)	L1	L1	L1	L1
Vision (Who? F3)	Vision	L2	L2	L3
Message (What? F2)	F1 – Using 3/3 process	Leadership Development	L3	L3
Baptism	F4 – Moving to Healthy Church	MAWL	Consultants to L3's	L4
Share Gospel	Short Term Discipleship	Gen Mapping	"Command" Skills	#NPL
Contatorsh	Long Term Discipleship	Iron on Iron (3x3)	Asking good questions	Fill segments
Houses of Peace Search	Church Function	Priesthood of Believers	Zero credit	
Intro Short Term Discipleship	Appointing Leaders	Release Authority	APEST expert	
	Church Identity	Bigger Vision	Diagnoses DNA Issues	
	One Another's	Identifying and Equipping Timothy's		
	Self –	Humility		
	Feeding	Administration		
	Correcting	Be able to handle scrutiny		
	Reproducing			
	Governing			
	5 Fields Strategy			

Key
- F1-4: Fields 1-4 from 4 Fields tool
- MAWL: Model, Assist, Watch, and Leave
- APEST: Apostle, Prophet, Evangelist, Shepherd, Teacher
- NPL: No Place Left
- 3/3: Look Back, Look Up, Look Forward

Bibliography

Chapter 1

[i] C.S. Lewis. *The Chronicles of Narnia: The Lion, the Witch and the Wardrobe.* United Kingdom: Geoffrey Bles, 1950

[ii] The Matrix. Warner Bros. Pictures, 2001. Film.

Chapter 2

[iii] Bruce Olson with James Lund. *Bruchko and the Motilone Miracle.* Lake Mary, Florida: Charisma House, 2006

[iv] Bruce Olson. *Bruchko.* Lake Mary, Florida: Charisma House, 1978

[v] Neil Cole. "The Life Transformation Group System by Neil Cole." CMA Resources. May 19, 2009. Accessed January 5, 2015. https://www.cmaresources.org/article/ltg

Chapter 3

[vi] *Grown Ups.* Sony Pictures Home Entertainment, 2010. Film.

[vii] 1989, Carol Davis, Tom Wolf and International Urban Institute – Leaf-Line Initiatives

Chapter 5

[viii] Dallas Willard. *The Divine Conspiracy: Rediscovering Our Hidden Life in God.* HarperOne, 1998

[ix] Dietrich Bonhoeffer. *The Cost of Discipleship.* New York: Touchstone, 1995

Chapter 6

[x] Neil Cole. *Organic Church: Growing Faith Where Life Happens.* San Francisco: Jossey-Bass, 2005

Chapter 7

[xi] Richard Pascale and Mark Milleman. *Surfing the Edge of Chaos: The Laws of Nature and the New Laws of Business*. Reed Business Information, Inc., 2000

[xii] Neil Cole. *Church 3.0: Upgrades for the Future of the Church*. San Francisco: Jossey-Bass, 2010

CPSIA information can be obtained
at www.ICGtesting.com
Printed in the USA
FSOW02n0408180118
43250FS